SUBCOMMITTEE ON GOVERNMENT EFFICIENCY AND FINANCIAL MANAGEMENT

TODD RUSSELL PLATTS, Pennsylvania, *Chairman*

MARSHA BLACKBURN, Tennessee
STEVEN C. LATOURETTE, Ohio
JOHN SULLIVAN, Oklahoma
CANDICE S. MILLER, Michigan
MICHAEL R. TURNER, Ohio

EDOLPHUS TOWNS, New York
PAUL E. KANJORSKI, Pennsylvania
MAJOR R. OWENS, New York
CAROLYN B. MALONEY, New York

EX OFFICIO

TOM DAVIS, Virginia

HENRY A. WAXMAN, California

MIKE HETTINGER, *Staff Director*
TABETHA MUELLER, *Professional Staff Member*

IDENTIFY, DISRUPT AND DISMANTLE: COORDINATING THE GOVERNMENT'S ATTACK ON TERRORIST FINANCING

JOINT HEARING

BEFORE THE

SUBCOMMITTEE ON TECHNOLOGY, INFORMATION POLICY, INTERGOVERNMENTAL RELATIONS AND THE CENSUS

AND THE

SUBCOMMITTEE ON GOVERNMENT EFFICIENCY AND FINANCIAL MANAGEMENT

OF THE

COMMITTEE ON GOVERNMENT REFORM

HOUSE OF REPRESENTATIVES

ONE HUNDRED EIGHTH CONGRESS

FIRST SESSION

DECEMEBER 15, 2003

Serial No. 108–140

Printed for the use of the Committee on Government Reform

Available via the World Wide Web: http://www.gpo.gov/congress/house
http://www.house.gov/reform

U.S. GOVERNMENT PRINTING OFFICE

93–428 PDF WASHINGTON : 2004

For sale by the Superintendent of Documents, U.S. Government Printing Office
Internet: bookstore.gpo.gov Phone: toll free (866) 512–1800; DC area (202) 512–1800
Fax: (202) 512–2250 Mail: Stop SSOP, Washington, DC 20402–0001

CONTENTS

	Page
Hearing held on December 15, 2003	1
Statement of:	
Forman, Marcy M., Deputy Assistant Director, Financial Investigations Division, U.S. Immigration and Customs Enforcement, U.S. Department of Homeland Security	51
Glass, George A., Director, Office of Terrorism Finance and Sanctions Policy, Bureau of Economic and Business Affairs, U.S. Department of State	26
Ross, Jeff, Senior Advisor, Executive Office for the Terrorist Financing/Financial Crimes, U.S. Department of the Treasury	7
Townsend, Bruce, Deputy Assistant Director, Office of Investigations, U.S. Secret Service, U.S. Department of Homeland Security	62
Whitehead, Carl, Special Agent in Charge, Tampa Office, Federal Bureau of Investigation, U.S. Department of Justice, accompanied by Frank J. Fabian, Unit Chief, Terrorist Financing Operations Section, Washington, DC	37
Letters, statements, etc., submitted for the record by:	
Forman, Marcy M., Deputy Assistant Director, Financial Investigations Division, U.S. Immigration and Customs Enforcement, U.S. Department of Homeland Security, prepared statement of	55
Glass, George A., Director, Office of Terrorism Finance and Sanctions Policy, Bureau of Economic and Business Affairs, U.S. Department of State, prepared statement of	29
Putnam, Hon. Adam H., a Representative in Congress from the State of Florida, prepared statement of	4
Ross, Jeff, Senior Advisor, Executive Office for the Terrorist Financing/Financial Crimes, U.S. Department of the Treasury, prepared statement of	11
Townsend, Bruce, Deputy Assistant Director, Office of Investigations, U.S. Secret Service, U.S. Department of Homeland Security, prepared statement of	64
Whitehead, Carl, Special Agent in Charge, Tampa Office, Federal Bureau of Investigation, U.S. Department of Justice, prepared statement of	40

IDENTIFY, DISRUPT AND DISMANTLE: CO-ORDINATING THE GOVERNMENT'S ATTACK ON TERRORIST FINANCING

MONDAY, DECEMBER 15, 2003

HOUSE OF REPRESENTATIVES, SUBCOMMITTEE ON TECHNOLOGY, INFORMATION POLICY, INTERGOVERNMENTAL RELATIONS AND THE CENSUS JOINT WITH THE SUBCOMMITTEE ON GOVERNMENT EFFICIENCY AND FINANCIAL MANAGEMENT, COMMITTEE ON GOVERNMENT REFORM,

Tampa, FL.

The subcommittees met, pursuant to notice, at 11:05 a.m., at the Tampa Port Authority Headquarters, 1st Floor Board Room, 1101 Channelside Drive, Tampa, FL, Hon. Adam Putnam (chairman of the Subcommittee on Technology, Information Policy, Intergovernmental Relations and the Census) presiding.

Present from the Subcommittee on Technology, Information Policy, Intergovernmental Relations and the Census: Representative Putnam.

Present from the Subcommittee on Government Efficiency and Financial Management: Representative Platts.

Staff present from the Subcommittee on Technology, Information Policy, Intergovernmental Relations and the Census: Robert Dix, staff director; John Hambel, senior counsel; Lori Martin, professional staff member; and Ursula Wojciechowski, clerk.

Staff present from the Subcommittee on Government Efficiency and Financial Management: Michael Hettinger, staff director; and Tabetha Mueller, professional staff member.

Mr. PUTNAM. A quorum being present, one from each subcommittee, a quorum in Congress, I guess, the joint hearing of the Subcommittee on Technology, Information Policy and Intergovernmental Relations and the Census, and the Subcommittee on Government Efficiency and Financial Management will come to order.

Good morning and welcome, everyone, to today's oversight hearing examining the Federal Government's efforts to combat money laundering and terrorist financing. Specifically we will be looking at how Federal agencies are coordinating their efforts to identify terrorist financing and the role of information technology in that endeavor.

On behalf of the Subcommittee on Technology, let me extend my appreciation to Mr. Platts and his able staff. It has been a model of congressional cooperation in setting aside turf and moving forward to get to the bottom of a very important issue.

And in a few moments I will be yielding to Mr. Platts for his opening remarks. He has been a leader in the money laundering issues, and his work on financial management has been outstanding.

I want to take a few minutes, though, to share a few thoughts from the perspective of the Technology Subcommittee that I have chaired this past year. One of the most effective ways to prevent future terrorist attacks on Americans and our allies is to disrupt the flow of the funds that finance the organizations. This is a complex challenge for several reasons. Federal agencies and State and local law enforcement must coordinate efforts with the private sector to identify transactions that raise suspicion. Considering the amount of information collected every day by banks and other financial institutions, this is a daunting task. In addition, the way terrorists move money through our financial institutions makes it even more difficult to identify and dismantle their funding schemes. We can't let the expense and difficulty of the task, though, keep us from pursuing and accomplishing this critical national security goal.

Federal and local law enforcement have worked together for years to uncover money laundering activity. Through the Bank Secrecy Act, the Money Laundering Control Act, and the National Money Laundering Strategy, Congress has given agencies the legislative tools to implement policies that help local law enforcement identify illicit financial activity. The focus of these efforts shifted after the attacks of September 11th.

While there are some similarities in the way money is moved in money laundering schemes, terrorist financing often finds its source in seemingly legitimate organizations. Illicit funds provided through money laundering can and do provide a ready source of money for terrorists. The full scope of terrorist financing, though, is much larger. One of the greatest challenges we face is how to improve the coordination and information sharing between Federal agencies such as Treasury, DHS, FBI and State Department with local authorities and private institutions.

While the use of emerging information technology can greatly assist in coordinating efforts, as well as identifying and tracking suspicious financial data, the right policy and trained personnel are essential in accomplishing this goal. And as always, we have to be mindful of the need to protect civil liberties as well as the privacy and physical security of the financial data that is being gathered and analyzed.

Congress and the administration have done extensive work already in setting sound policy to assist in the task of shutting down terrorist financing. Enactment of the U.S. Patriot Act and creation of the Department of Homeland Security in response to September 11th has required Federal agencies to alter the way financial crimes are defined and targeted with an emphasis on much-needed coordination.

Congress will also be reassessing the National Money Laundering Strategy in the coming year to determine whether and how it should be renewed, since it is currently authorized only through 2003.

And, finally, it is critical that Congress continue to exercise its oversight responsibilities as agencies learn to leverage resources and utilize information technology effectively and efficiently. This is an issue that is near and dear to the Tampa Bay area, with the Sami al-Arian case at the University of South Florida as well as other incidents in our area.

And it is important and appropriate that we hold this field hearing here in Tampa where we have a number of local and Federal law enforcement agencies who have firsthand experience in dealing with this terribly complex task. And we appreciate certainly Chairman Platts' willingness to fly to Florida from Pennsylvania in the dead of winter to be with us and join us.

And we would certainly be remiss if we did not acknowledge the tremendous holiday gift to all mankind that occurred yesterday courtesy of the American soldiers and sailors and marines and airmen who delivered Saddam Hussein to the world to stand trial and find justice for the crimes that he has committed against the Iraqi people.

With that, Mr. Platts, thank you so much for your assistance, and welcome to Florida.

[The prepared statement of Hon. Adam H. Putnam follows:]

Committee on Government Reform

Subcommittee on Technology, Information Policy, Intergovernmental Relations and the Census

Congressman Adam Putnam, Chairman

OVERSIGHT HEARING
STATEMENT BY ADAM PUTNAM, CHAIRMAN

Hearing topic: ***Identify, Disrupt, and Dismantle: Coordinating the Government's Attack on Terrorist Financing***

Monday, December 15, 2003
11:00 a.m.
Tampa Port Authority Headquarters
Tampa, Florida

OPENING STATEMENT

One of the most effective ways to prevent future terrorist attacks on Americans and our allies is to disrupt the flow of the funds that finance terrorist organizations. This is a complex challenge for several reasons: Federal agencies and state and local law enforcement must coordinate efforts with the private sector to identify transactions that should raise suspicion. Considering the amount of information collected everyday by banks and other financial institutions, this is a daunting task. In addition, the way terrorists move money through our financial institutions makes it more difficult to identify and dismantle their funding schemes. However, we cannot let the expense and difficulty of the task keep us from pursuing and accomplishing this critical national security goal.

Federal and local law enforcement have worked together for years to uncover money laundering activity. Through the Bank Secrecy Act, The Money Laundering Control Act and the National Money Laundering Strategy, Congress has given agencies the legislative tools to implement policies that help law enforcement identify illicit financial activity. The focus of these efforts shifted a little after the attacks of 9/11. While there are some similarities in the way money is moved in money laundering schemes, terrorist financing often finds its source in seemingly legitimate organizations. Illicit funds provided through money laundering can and do provide a ready source of money for terrorists. The full scope of terrorist financing, however, is much larger.

One of the greatest challenges we face is how to improve coordination and information sharing between Federal agencies, such as Treasury, DHS, FBI and State Department, with local authorities and private institutions. While the use of emerging information technology can greatly assist in coordinating efforts as well as identifying and tracking suspicious financial data, the right policy and trained personnel are essential in accomplishing our goal, and as always, we must be mindful of the need to protect civil liberties as well as the privacy and physical security of financial data being gathered and analyzed.

Congress and the Administration have done extensive work already in setting sound policy to assist in the task of shutting down terrorist financing. Enactment of the USA PATRIOT Act and creation of the Department of Homeland Security (DHS) in response to 9/11 has required federal agencies to alter the way financial crimes are defined and targeted, with an emphasis on the much needed coordination between agencies. Congress will also be reassessing the National Money Laundering Strategy in the coming year to determine whether and how it should be renewed since it is currently authorized only through 2003. Finally, it is critical that Congress continue to exercise its oversight responsibilities as agencies learn to leverage resources and utilize information technology effectively and efficiently.

Mr. PLATTS. Thank you, Mr. Chairman. It is great to be here with you. And I echo your sentiments about the appropriateness of our subcommittees working together as we are going to be talking about cooperation within our law enforcement communities on terrorist financing. It is certainly appropriate as a body that Congress try to show cooperation and coordination as well.

And I also echo your sentiments on the great news that we got yesterday. And yesterday was about capturing Saddam Hussein, the person. Today it is about how we cutoff the money that flows to the people like Saddam and help funnel the terrorist attacks, whether it be against Iraqis, Americans or other peace-loving citizens around the world.

So I appreciate your hosting today's hearing. It is always important, I think, for us when we have field hearings, a chance to get out into our communities and meet with follow public servants as well as for citizens to maybe see government in action a little closer to home. And this hearing certainly is an important one, and maybe, with the timing of yesterday's capture of Saddam, all the more important that we are here today.

We certainly know that financial crime is the functional equivalent of a war industry for terrorists. Money provides the life blood for acts of terror. Criminal activity we typically associate with money laundering, smuggling, drug sales, counterfeiting offer terrorists a ready source of funds. The scope of terrorist financing, however, is unfortunately much larger than that.

Legitimate charities, as was experienced here in south Florida, nonprofit corporations, think tanks have all funneled millions of dollars through the U.S. banking system to fund terrorist activities. Many of the organizations have earned tax-exempt status from the IRS. This new reality driven home by the tragic attacks on September 11th require a new focus in the war on financial crime. While the source and destination of funding may differ, the mechanism used to disguise funds for terrorist organizations are similar to those used by drug traffickers and criminal organizations.

With tools provided by the USA Patriot Act and the strategic efforts that have been in play to fight drug cartels, the Federal Government has sharpened its focus and promoted unprecedented coordination among law enforcement entities and foreign governments. And I know we are going to hear much about that coordination here today.

It is difficult to quantify the success of the Federal Government's attack on terrorist financing. While we know that millions of dollars in assets have been frozen around the world, the ultimate goal of terrorist financing investigations is the disruption of the flow of money, a result much more difficult to quantify.

The United States has sought and received unprecedented support from other countries in overhauling the laws governing the international financial system and in designating entities as supporters of terror. And we have increased transparency and vigilance in the private sector. Our best weapon to attack money laundering and terrorist financing threats is a comprehensive and coordinated response. In this case, efficiency and effectiveness are not just good government rhetoric, they have the potential to save lives by preventing terrorist attacks.

Recognizing the need for coordination efforts, as you referenced, in 1998 Congress mandated the development of an annual National Money Laundering Strategy. Much has changed since that time. Five years later, the National Money Laundering Strategy is up for reauthorization. We in Congress have a responsibility to take a hard look at whether this type of approach is the most effective.

We need to be sure that our dedicated law enforcement and other government officials continue to have the tools they need to be responsive to changes in technology and methodology, and the flexibility to keep up with emerging challenges. We must continue to enhance our ability to identify and eliminate various avenues used to launder money, whether it be for drug traffickers, criminal organizations or terrorists.

And we certainly today have a great panel of witnesses who are on the front lines of the war on terrorism and on terrorist financing. I want to thank each of you for your participation here today, but especially for your service to our Nation and our fellow citizens. We are blessed because of your service of you and your colleagues, and I certainly look forward to your testimony and appreciated the weekend reading you provided in providing that testimony to us ahead of time and allowing us to have an even more informed dialog here today. So thank you, Mr. Chairman.

Mr. PUTNAM. Thank you, Mr. Chairman.

At this time, as is the custom with the Government Reform Committee, we will swear in our witnesses. I would ask the panel and anyone accompanying the panel who will be providing supplementary information to please rise and raise your right hands.

[Witnesses sworn.]

Mr. PUTNAM. Note for the record that all of the witnesses responded in the affirmative.

We have notified the public that we will be here about 2 hours. We typically allow 5 minutes for opening statements. I think, considering the size of the subcommittee and the importance of the topic, if you go a little bit over, we are certainly not going to hit the eject button on you. But we would ask you to summarize your statements in 5 minutes or as close to that as possible so we can get into the question and answers and dialog.

Our first witness for this hearing is Jeff Ross. Mr. Ross is the senior advisor for the Executive Office for Terrorist Financing and Financial Crimes with the Department of the Treasury. Mr. Ross serves as senior advisor in the area of money laundering and terrorist financing in this newly created office. That office, reporting to the Deputy Secretary of the Treasury, has been charged with coordinating and leading Treasury's multifaceted efforts to identify and attack systematically terrorist financing, money laundering and financial crimes, as well as spearhead the effort to identify and freeze Iraqi assets looted by the former regime.

Mr. Ross, you have $750,000 in additional assets thanks to the capture of Saddam Hussein. Welcome to the subcommittee.

STATEMENT OF JEFF ROSS, SENIOR ADVISOR, EXECUTIVE OFFICE FOR THE TERRORIST FINANCING/FINANCIAL CRIMES, U.S. DEPARTMENT OF THE TREASURY

Mr. ROSS. Thank you, Mr. Chairman. Thank you both.

Preliminarily, this hearing is not about his capture, but I will note for the record that Mr. Hussein felt that there were four essentials for his survival: a ventilator fan, an air pipe, a pistol, and, as you correctly noted, $750,000 in crisp U.S. $100 bills. So "follow the money where the money goes" even as of yesterday was pointed out again.

Good morning, and thank you again for the invitation. I have prepared a formal written testimony, which I would appreciate if the subcommittee would accept into the record.

Mr. PUTNAM. Mr. Ross, before you begin, could you pull the mic a little bit closer, or clip it to your tie or something? We want to make sure that the reporter picks it up.

Mr. ROSS. OK. Preliminarily I would like to thank these committees and the Congress for the new and enhanced tools which the Congress has given the executive branch to identify and attack terrorist financing, money laundering, and other financial crimes. I assure you we will use those powers aggressively, but judiciously.

Money serves both as the fuel for terror, narcotrafficking and organized crime, as well as a significant vulnerability. Money flows leave a signature and audit trail; provide a road map, which, once discovered, might well prove the best single means for identification and capture of terrorists and their facilitators and other criminals. If we and our international partners can identify, follow and stop the money, we will have gone a long way to destroy this infrastructure.

The Treasury strongly believes that resources devoted to fighting money laundering and financial crimes reap benefits far beyond merely addressing the underlying financial crimes that they are targeting. The terrorist financiers, money launderers and other financial criminals leave footprints in the global system, and these footprints lead in two directions, both forward to identify future perpetrators and facilitators and backward to identify supporting entities and individuals. Additionally, it leads to information which would allow for asset recovery.

To pursue this following-the-money approach, last March Treasury established the Executive Office, which the chairman was kind enough to describe. It is a small office with a lot of responsibilities, the last of which is the search for and attempt to repatriate as much of the Iraqi assets as Hussein looted as is possible.

A quick mention about Tampa. I agree, this is a fitting venue for this hearing. Tampa law enforcement has been and is on the cutting edge of investigating and prosecuting both, Mr. Whitehead. More than a decade ago the BCCI case filed here in Tampa revealed the global implications of money laundering, and that case has become a byword for the complexity and global reach of international money launderers.

On the terrorist financing front, as we have already heard, the Sami al-Arian case, which is a principal case here, and terrorist financing was a principal component of the charges in that case.

Just as money laundering involves the placement, movement and integration of criminal proceeds in the legitimate financial system, the horrific end results of terrorist activities require the raising, movement and use of large volumes of funds. The terrorist act itself cannot be accomplished without a sophisticated financial and operational infrastructure that costs millions, if not tens of millions, of dollars. This infrastructure—including purchasing safe houses, martyrs' family support, recruitment costs, indoctrination costs, logistical and personnel training and support, and finally the purchase of weapons—must be exploited.

The committees have asked for some examples of successes in this war. Perhaps the most visible weapon on the financial front of the war against terrorism has been the public designation of terrorists and their support network coupled with freezing their assets under Executive Order 13–224, put out by the President September 24, 2001. To date, 344 individuals and entities, including 23 charities, have been designated, or over $136 million frozen worldwide.

However, numbers designated and funds frozen must never be construed as the ultimate barometer of the effectiveness of our financial war on terrorism. Only a small measure of success is counted in the dollars frozen. The larger balance is found in the changes that the global attacks have cost in the methodologies of raising, moving and using the financing of terror. All engaged in terror financing systems are at increased risk and scrutiny, domestically by the Patriot Act, in Saudi Arabia by increased scrutiny on charities, in the Middle East and Pakistan on remittances, and the alternate remittance system. Compelled changes in financing methodologies disrupt systems, increase the risk of detection and may ultimately dry up the pipelines themselves.

Other noteworthy achievements: Almost 700 terror-related accounts blocked worldwide, 100 in the United States; 172 countries' blocking orders in force against assets of terrorists; 80 countries have introduced new terror-related legislation; 84 countries now have FinCEN-equivalent financial intelligence units.

Treasury, with Department of State, established a $5 million Treasury counterterrorism fund. As we sit here, there has been created and there is in place an FBI-IRS CI training capability in Saudi Arabia working on the financial side. IRS CI has 41 interagency SAR review teams, including one operating right here in Tampa as we speak, download and review 140,000 SARs annually for possible leads to terrorist financing. The Financial Action Task Force has issued special recommendations. There have been—40 countries accepted an Abu Dhabi Declaration on Hawalas, which is an important alternative remittance system, international attack.

Since passage of the Patriot Act, 14,000 money service businesses have registered with FinCEN, very important, now subject to SAR reporting. There have been a number of Department of Justice-initiated cases, which are described in the formal testimony, and I will leave the FBI and Justice to wax on those.

Second component, the 2003 National Money Laundering Strategy. The strategy was released last month, has three overarching goals: Safeguarding the national financial system for money laundering and terrorist financing; enhance the U.S. Government's ability to identify, investigate and prosecute money laundering organizations; and ensure effective regulation.

The core principle of this strategy is enhancing our ongoing efforts to combat money laundering by using interagency approaches such as HIFCAs, OCDETFs, SAR review team and HIDTAs. We also are using our asset forfeiture laws. The Treasury Executive

Office for Asset Forfeiture reports that fiscal year 2003 receipts into the Treasury fund exceeded $250 million, which is a 45 percent increase over the fiscal year 2002 receipts.

Through OFAC we are implementing the specially designated Narcotics Trafficker Program. We are working on the Foreign Narcotics Drug Kingpin Act program to attack drug money launderers. We have identified, through cases, clear links between Colombia and terrorism and narcotrafficking.

Regulatory effectiveness. Patriot Act mandates the greatest numbers of substantial changes to the U.S. anti-money-laundering regulatory regime in recent memory. Among things we have done is we have closed off our financial borders to foreign shell banks, required additional due diligence for correspondent accounts, required foreign banks with correspondent accounts to identify a person for service of process. We have required U.S. financial institutions to establish customer identification and verification.

Two points in the Patriot Act I would like to mention very briefly. Patriot Act section 311 enables the Secretary to protect the U.S. financial system against specific terrorist financing and money laundering threats posed by foreign financial institutions, accounts or even jurisdictions. The mere possibility of these designations has caused the nations to make changes to their legal and regulatory regimes and enhance the global anti-money-laundering and terrorist financing infrastructure.

Another provision is 314(a), which permits FinCEN to make contact with over 29,000 U.S. financial institutions in one fell swoop. It permits law enforcement agencies quickly to locate the accounts and transactions of those suspected of significant money laundering or the financing of terror. Since it was inaugurated last February, it has supported 64 terrorism/terrorist financing cases and 124 money laundering cases. Three indictments have resulted, in part, from searches made under this system, 407 grand jury subpoenas, 11 search warrants.

Very quickly on technology, criminals benefit from enhancements in technology, as both these subcommittees are well aware. So does U.S. law enforcement. Technology holds one of the keys to our success in the financial war on terrorism. Appendix H of the National Money Laundering Strategy has a long report on terrorist financing on-line. It identifies how we are trying to identify and attack it.

IRS CI has a pilot counterterrorism project that is utilizing all Treasury data bases as well as tax-related—protected tax information, to support FBI Joint Terrorism Task Forces.

Finally, FinCEN since September 11 has supported 2,692 terrorist investigations. The terror hotline has resulted in 789 tips. FinCEN has received over 2,842 SARs possibly related to terrorist financing.

Technology works in two directions. We at the Treasury are trying to work from our side. Thank you very much.

Mr. PUTNAM. Thank you, Mr. Ross.

[The prepared statement of Mr. Ross follows:]

DEPARTMENT OF THE TREASURY
OFFICE OF PUBLIC AFFAIRS

Embargoed Until Delivery
December 15, 2003

Contact: Tara Bradshaw
(202) 622-2014

Testimony of Lee Jeffrey Ross, Jr
Senior Advisor, Executive Office for Terrorist Financing & Financial Crimes
U.S. Department of the Treasury
Before the
House Committee on Government Reform
Joint Subcommittees on Government Efficiency and Financial Management and on Technology, Information Policy, Intergovernmental Affairs and the Census
December 15, 2003

Chairmen Putnam and Platts and distinguished members of the Committee, permit me to begin by thanking you for inviting me to testify today about Treasury and other government achievements in our efforts, at home and abroad, to identify, disrupt and dismantle sources of terrorist financing; the *2003 National Money Laundering Strategy* with special emphasis on interagency coordination; and, the United States Government efforts to use technology to identify and attack terrorist financing.

Money serves both as the fuel for the enterprises of terror, narco-trafficking and organized crime, as well as a significant vulnerability. Money flows leave a signature, an audit trail, and provide a road map of terror, money laundering, and organized crime which, once discovered, might well prove the best single means of identification and capture of terrorists and their facilitators, narco-trafficking cartels and infrastructure and organized crime worldwide. Thus, stopping the flow of money to terrorists, narco-traffickers and other organized criminals may be one of the very best ways we have of stopping the supported criminal activity altogether. If we and our international partners can follow and stop the money, we will have gone a long way toward destroying the infrastructure supporting these criminals.

Thus, the Department of the Treasury strongly believes that "targeting the money," especially when applied on a systemic basis, is a key pursuit, in and of itself, to identify and attack all kinds of other criminal activity, including the financing of terrorism, narcotics trafficking, white collar crime including securities frauds, organized crime, and public corruption. We believe that resources devoted to fighting money laundering and financial crimes reap benefits far beyond merely addressing the underlying financial crimes they directly target. Financial investigations lead upstream to those who are generating the underlying financial crimes, as well as downstream to provide a roadmap to those who facilitate the criminal activity, such as broker-dealers, bankers, lawyers and accountants. These investigations lead to the recovery and forfeiture of illegally-obtained assets as well as facilitating property both at home and abroad.

To pursue this "follow the money" approach in the Department's efforts to combat terrorist financing, money laundering, and other financial crimes, on March 3, 2003, the Department of the Treasury established the Executive Office for Terrorist Financing and Financial Crimes (EOTF/FC). EOTF/FC, supervised by a Deputy Assistant Secretary who reports to the Deputy Secretary of the Treasury, works closely with other Treasury offices, other Federal and state government agencies, foreign government counterparts, and the private sector to prevent terrorists, money launderers, criminal tax evaders and other financial criminals from abusing the domestic and international financial systems, and to identify, block, and dismantle sources of terrorist financing, money laundering and other financial crimes. Since March, EOTF/FC has been leading the United States Government's interagency and international effort to identify, freeze and return Iraqi assets, including both governmental funds and those looted by the former regime.

The Treasury Department is grateful to this Committee and the Congress for the additional resources, authorities, and support given to the Executive Branch to assist Treasury attack terrorist financial networks and money launderers. Of particular importance to these efforts, the USA PATRIOT Act expands the law enforcement and intelligence community's ability to access and share critical financial information regarding terrorist investigations. We at the Treasury have used and will continue to use the enhanced powers given us aggressively, but judiciously, and have made every effort to work directly with our private financial sector partners in these efforts.

Tampa-Anti-Money Laundering/Terrorist Financing

It is altogether fitting that this hearing on money laundering and terrorist financing is occurring in Tampa. Tampa law enforcement has been and is on the cutting edge of investigating and prosecuting both. More than a decade ago, the Bank of Commerce and Credit International (BCCI) case, filed here in Tampa, established the global implications of money laundering. The "BCCI" case has become a by-word for the complexity, global reach and potential abuse of financial institutions and systems by money launderers. Nor is large scale money laundering restricted to international businessmen. Not too long ago, in Tampa, Haywood "Don" Hall was convicted of using his Greater Ministries International Church to bilk more than 18,000 "investors," and launder almost $500 million in a classic *Ponzi* scheme. This past February, an indictment here was returned charging more than $18 million in a securities fraud and money laundering scheme.

According to the U.S. Department of Justice's Bureau of Justice Statistics Report, issued this past July, Tampa ranks sixth in the nation in money laundering investigations (55) referred for prosecution in 2001. FinCEN reports that from January 1, 2001 to October 31, 2003, Tampa banks and other depository institutions filed some 1410 SARs reporting 1557 possible violations. One SAR reported possible terrorist financing. Money service businesses have had to file SARs since January 1, 2002. From that date until October 31, 2003, some 190 such SARs were filed. Three of those SARs reported possible terrorist financing.

On the terror financing front, the Department of Justice's February 2003 RICO indictment here of Sami al-Arian and others on fifty counts, including a conspiracy to provide material support to the Palestinian Islamic Jihad, and a conspiracy to make and receive contribution to and from a specially designated terrorists, is of immense importance and points out the importance of using the money trail to find criminal conduct.

I. Attacking Terrorist Financing

The financial trail left by terrorists and their facilitators represents a vulnerability that must be pursued and exploited. It is crucial to remember that the horrific end result of terrorist activities require the raising, movement and use of large volumes of funds. The terrorist act itself, no matter how basic and inexpensive, cannot be accomplished without a sophisticated financial and operational infrastructure that collectively cost millions, if not tens of millions of dollars. Terrorism's financial and operational infrastructure--"safe havens" that must be purchased, "martyrs" families that must be supported, the costs of indoctrination, logistical and personnel training and support and the costs of medical clinics and schools that some groups use to win support and recruits, and finally the purchase of the weapons-- represent a significant vulnerability that we and our international partners must attack. The terrorist leaves bloody footprints in the global financial systems, and these footprints must be pursued forward to identify future perpetrators and facilitators, and backwards to identify and dismantle supporting entities and individuals.

In the United States and overseas, the war on terrorist financing is being waged via the following:

(i)an Executive Order using the powers granted by the Congress through the International Emergency Economic Powers Act that raises the standards of conduct and due diligence of financial intermediaries, and explicitly targets underwriters of terror for the freezing of their assets;

(ii) UN Security Council resolutions and conventions that internationalize asset freezes and mandate the criminalization of terrorist financing;

(iii)the formal designation by the Secretary of State of foreign terrorist organizations, resulting in the freezing of assets and other sanctions;

(iv) more scrutiny at the gateway to U.S. financial markets that has been provided under the USA PATRIOT Act;

(v) law enforcement criminal investigations, prosecutions, and foreign intelligence operations aimed at terrorist supporters and terrorist financiers;

(vi) extensive diplomatic efforts, including the engagement of central bankers and finance ministries, to champion the wisdom of and need for international vigilance against terrorist financing and the taking of appropriate action to address it;

(vii) outreach to the private sector for assistance in the identification, location and apprehension of terrorists and their bankers; and,

(viii) bilateral and multilateral efforts to build laws and systems that will help prevent terrorists from corrupting the financial system in developing countries around the globe, followed by training missions dispatched to those countries to help their officials strengthen and administer those laws.

One of the most visible and effective weapons on the financial front of the war has been the public designation of terrorists and their support network coupled with the freezing of their assets. The Executive Order imposing economic sanctions under the International Emergency Economic Powers Act permits the public designation of not only terrorists and terrorist organizations, but also supporters, facilitators and underwriters of terror as well. Once these individuals and entities are designated, this order freezes the assets of the designee held by U.S. persons. Action under this order is not "criminal" and does not require proof beyond a reasonable doubt. Designation accomplishes many results:

(i) shutting down the pipeline by which designated parties moved money and operated financially in the mainstream financial sectors;

(ii) informing third parties who may be unwittingly financing terrorist activity of their association with supporters of terrorism;

(iii) deterring undesignated parties that might otherwise be willing to finance terrorist activity;

(iv) exposing terrorist financing "money trails" that may generate leads to previously unknown terrorist cells and financiers;

(v) forcing terrorists to use more costly informal means of financing their activities;

(vi) supporting our diplomatic efforts to strengthen other countries' capacities to combat terrorist financing; and

(vii) supporting criminal prosecutions for willful violations of the requirements of IEEPA.

To date, some 344 individuals and entities have been designated, and over $136 million frozen worldwide. Numbers designated and funds frozen, however, must never be construed as the ultimate barometer of the effectiveness of our financial war on terrorism. Only a small measure of success in the campaign is counted in the dollars of frozen accounts. The larger balance is found in the changes that the global attacks have caused in the methodologies of raising, moving and using the financing of terror. All engaged in terror financing systems are at increased risk and scrutiny—at home from enhanced regulatory scrutiny mandated in the USA PATRIOT Act, in Saudi Arabia and elsewhere from the increased scrutiny given to charities, in the Middle East and Pakistan on the use of alternative remittance systems, and elsewhere. Compelled changes in financing methodologies disrupt systems, increase the risk of detection, and ultimately dry up the financial pipelines.

In addition, the Secretary of State, in consultation with the Secretary of Treasury and the Attorney General, can formally designate terrorist groups as Foreign Terrorist Organizations. (FTOs). Such designations, authorized under the 1996 Antiterrorism and Effective Death Penalty Act, result in the freezing of assets in the United States of designated groups, and make it a criminal offense for U.S. persons to provide funds or other forms of material support to the designated groups. Members as well as leaders of FTOS are made ineligible for visas to the United States. Currently 36 groups are designated as FTOs.

The Subcommittees have asked the Department to address the importance of interagency cooperation and coordination in our war on terrorist financiers. Terrorist financing is a complicated and multi-dimensional problem that implicates a range of legal, regulatory, financial, intelligence and law enforcement interests. It is axiomatic then that any successful attack on systemic terrorist financing must adopt vigorous interagency (law enforcement. regulatory, diplomatic, intelligence, defense, as appropriate) consultation and cooperation.

To accomplish this result, shortly after the attacks of September 11, in furtherance of developing and implementing a coordinated interagency attack on terrorist financing, the National Security Council established a Policy Coordinating Committee on Terrorist Financing. The purpose of the Committee is to (i) recommend strategic policy direction to the National Security Council on issues relating to terrorist financing; (ii) vet and approve proposed public action against targeted terrorists and terrorist financiers; and (iii) coordinate the United States' efforts on issues relating to terrorist financing. The Treasury Department has chaired that Committee since October 2001.

The Committee structure ensures that we are working toward achieving the goals of the committee; however, we have purposefully kept the process flexible, informal, collaborative and iterative. It is a process that has worked well to vet and coordinate proposed policy, diplomatic, and other actions by the United States on the financial front of the war on terrorism.

From the domestic law enforcement perspective, IRS-CI participates on the FBI's JTTFs and the Attorney General's Anti-terrorism Advisory Councils, concentrating on the financial infrastructure and fundraising activities of domestic and international terrorist groups. IRS-CI works closely with the FBI, other law enforcement agencies, the Department of Treasury, and the Department of Justice (DOJ) to disrupt and dismantle the financial components of terrorist organizations. IRS-CI places considerable emphasis and focus on the use of alternative remittance systems and tax-exempt organizations suspected of facilitating the movement of funds used to support terrorism. IRS-CI and FinCEN also participate in the interagency Foreign

Terrorist Asset Targeting Group (FTAT-G) that vets possible terrorist financing targets. The FTAT-G reports to the PCC on Terrorist Financing.

Terrorist Financing Successes

Among the noteworthy achievements in this area are the following:

- On September 24, 2001, President Bush issued Executive Order 13244, "Blocking Property and Prohibiting Transactions with Persons Who Commit, Threaten to Commit, or Support Terrorism." Section 1 of the Order states: "All property and interests in property of the following persons. . .that are in the United States or that hereafter come within the United States, or that hereafter come within the possession or control of United States persons are blocked."
- 344 terrorist-related entities and individuals, including 23 charities, are currently designated by the United States pursuant to this E.O. The international community has frozen over $136.8 million in over 1400 accounts and transfers worldwide. $64 million of additional terrorist-related assets have been seized worldwide.
- Almost 700 terror-related accounts blocked worldwide including 100 in United States have been blocked.
- 172 countries have blocking orders in force against the assets of terrorists, and 52 countries have submitted names to the United Nations Sanctions Committee for designation.
- 80 countries have introduced new terror-related legislation, and 84 countries now have established Financial Intelligence Units.
- On November 13, 2002, the Department of the Treasury, with the Department of State, established a Counter Terrorist Financing Rewards Program, funded with $5 million from Treasury's Counter-Terrorism Fund.
- Creation of, and FBI/IRS-CI training for, the Saudi Arabia/United States Joint Task Force on Terrorist Financing.
- Use of IRS-CI's 41 interagency SAR Review teams, including one in Tampa, to download and review approximately 140,000 SARs annually for possible leads to terrorist financing.
- November 2003 suspension by the IRS and the Department of the Treasury of tax-exempt status of the previously-designated Global Relief Foundation, Inc., the Benevolence International Foundation, Inc. and the Holy Land Foundation for Relief and Development.
- The Departments of State, Treasury and Justice also established an interagency Terrorist Financing Working Group, chaired by the State Department, to coordinate government efforts to identify, prioritize and assess those countries vulnerable to terrorist exploitation. To date, groups of experts, including DOJ prosecutors, interagency law enforcement and regulatory members, have provided extensive on-the-ground assessments to 16 countries to help build or reinforce their terrorist financing/money laundering regimes.
- On October 31, 2001, the FATF issued the Eight Special Recommendations on Terrorist Financing, including criminalizing the financing of terrorism, freezing and confiscating of terrorist assets, requiring SAR reporting relating to terrorist financing, extending anti-

money laundering requirements to alternative remittance systems, ensuring that non-profit organizations cannot be misused for terrorist financing, and requiring financial institutions to include accurate and meaningful originator information in wire transfers.

- Development and publication by Treasury of voluntary "best practices" for U.S. charities.
- May 2002 acceptance by over 40 countries of the *Abu Dhabi Declaration on Hawalas.*
- On October 1, 2002, FinCEN's secure link with certain financial institutions (PACS) became operational.
- Since passage of the USA PATRIOT Act, more than 14,000 money service businesses, including money remitters have registered with FinCEN, and are now subject to SAR reporting.
- *U.S.-Saudi Joint Designations* --On March 11, 2002, the United States participated in its first joint designation of a terrorist supporter. Acting with Saudi Arabia, we jointly designated the Somalia and Bosnia-Herzegovina offices of Al Haramain, a Saudi-based NGO linked to al Qaida, and jointly forwarded the names of these organizations to the UN Sanctions Committee for inclusion under the UNSCR 1333/1390 list. On September 9, 2002, the United States and Saudi Arabia jointly referred to the Sanctions Committee Wa'el Hamza Julaidan, an associate of Usama bin Laden and al Qaida supporter.
- *G7 Joint Designation*--On April 19, 2002, the United States and the other G7 members jointly designated nine individuals and one organization. Most of these groups were European-based al Qaida organizers and terrorism financiers. Because of their al Qaida links, all ten names were forwarded to the UN Sanctions Committee for inclusion under the UNSCR 1333/1390 list.
- *U.S.-Italy Joint Designation*--On August 29, 2002, the United States and Italy jointly designated 11 individuals linked to the Salafist Group for Call and Combat designated in the original U.S. Annex to E.O. 13224, and 14 entities that are part of the Nada/Nasreddin financial network run by two terrorist financiers designated on earlier E.O. 13224 lists.
- *Jemaa Islamiyya Leaders* (JI)--In October 2002, fifty (50) nations combined jointly to designate JI), an al-Qaida related terrorist network in Southeast Asia, as a terrorist group -- the most widespread show of support of any terrorist designation to date.
- OAS/CICAD/CICTE: In November 2003, the Group of Experts to Control Money Laundering of the Organization of American States' Inter-American Drug Abuse Control Commission (OAS/CICAD), during a session chaired by the Department of Justice, prepared final draft model provisions to guide legislators in adopting criminal offenses of terrorist financing, mechanisms to immediately block terrorist assets in accordance with United Nations Security Council resolutions, and to control alternative remittance systems. The OAS Inter-American Committee Against Terrorism (CICTE) is planning training for prosecutors and judges in member countries on terrorism and terrorist financing.
- Since September 11, 2001, the Department of Justice has prosecuted over 45 individuals for "providing material support" to terrorists or for operating illegal transmitting businesses which illegally transferred millions of dollars to Iraq and other Middle Eastern countries. These cases include:

- On February 19, 2003, a Federal grand jury indicted Professor Sami Al-Arian, three overseas leaders of Palestinian Islamic Jihad (PIJ), and four members of the Tampa, Florida, PIJ cell headed by Al-Arian, for conspiracy to commit racketeering, murder, and for knowingly providing material support to PIJ, a designated foreign terrorist organization (FTO). PIJ, based in Syria and Lebanon, has, as part of the Palestinian-Israeli conflict, engaged in a campaign of suicide bombings and armed attacks that have killed hundreds of innocent people, including American visiting, working or studying in Israel.

- A recent North Carolina-based multi-agency cigarette smuggling case revealed a massive cigarette smuggling and tax evasion scheme, in which Lebanese members of a Charlotte, North Carolina, Hizballah Cell were smuggling untaxed cigarettes from North Carolina to Michigan and using the proceeds to provide financial support and military equipment to terrorists in Beirut, Lebanon. The case culminated in Federal prosecutors convicting 18 people for material support of terrorism and other crimes involved in the smuggling scheme. The lead defendant, Mohammed Hammoud, was sentenced in February 2003, to 155 years in prison.

- In March 2003, federal prosecutors in Brooklyn unsealed indictments against two recently-extradited from Germany Yemeni nationals, including Mohammed Ali-Hassan al-Moayad who boasted that he had provided some $20 million to Usama bin Laden, for engaging in a plot to raise funds from U.S. sources for al Qaida and HAMAS.

- In August 2003, a criminal complaint was filed against Hemant Lakhani and Yehuda Abraham, a New York diamond merchant. The complaint charged Lakhani with material support for terrorist and Abraham with conspiracy to operate an illegal money remitter. Both defendants allegedly were apprehended as a result of an FBI "sting" operation in which an alleged terrorist attempted to purchase 50 shoulder-fired missiles for a terrorist organization.

- On December 18, 2002, a Federal grand jury in Dallas, Texas, returned a superceding indictment (following an initial indictment in February 2002), charging Ghassen Elashi, the chairman of the Holy Land Foundation for Relief and Development and HAMAS leader Mousa Abu Marzook, the Holy Land Foundation's most significant early donor, for prohibited financial dealings with terrorists.

- On February 10, 2003, Enaam Arnaout, Executive Director of the Benevolence International Foundation, pleaded guilty in Chicago to operating his charity as a Racketeer Influenced Corrupt Organization (RICO) enterprise and failing to tell donors that their money was being used to support violent *jihad*. In August, he was sentenced to more than 11 years imprisonment and restitution to the United Nations High Commission on Refugees in the amount of $315,000.

- On February 26, 2003, a Federal prosecutor unsealed criminal charges and brought criminal cases against persons in Syracuse, New York and Boise, Idaho, for allegedly financing terrorism through charities known as "Help the Needy" and "The Islamic Association of North America."

II. 2003 National Money Laundering Strategy (2003 Strategy)

Last month, the Department, in close cooperation with the Department of Justice, and numerous other agencies and departments, released the *2003 Strategy*. The *2003 Strategy* provides a framework for the U.S. government's ongoing commitment to attack money laundering and terrorist financing on all fronts.

The 2003 Strategy has three overarching Goals:

Safeguard the International Financial System from Money Laundering and Terrorist Financing. Through a variety of bilateral and multilateral means, the U.S. will continue to promote international coöperation in using intelligence, law enforcement, and administrative powers--including strengthening the legal, financial, and regulatory infrastructure of countries around the world--to better secure the international financial system against abuse by terrorist financiers and non-terrorist criminal organizations.

Enhance the United States Government's Ability to Identify, Investigate, and Prosecute Major Money Laundering Organizations and Systems. Money laundering must be made a primary--not merely an ancillary--component of any attack on substantive crimes that generate illicit proceeds and/or that facilitate terrorism.

Ensure Effective Regulation. Among other things, the U.S. will continue to strengthen and refine the anti-money laundering regulatory regime for all financial institutions; improve the effectiveness of anti-money laundering controls through greater communication, guidance, and information sharing with the private sector; and enhance regulatory compliance and enforcement efforts.

These Goals are focused on six key objectives:

- ***Blocking terrorist and illicit assets and cutting off worldwide channels of terrorist and illicit funding.***
- ***Establishing and promoting international standards to be adopted by countries to ensure that their financial systems are adequately protected from abuse by terrorist and other criminal organizations.***
- ***Ensuring that countries throughout the world consistently implement these international standards.***

- ***Focusing efforts on financing mechanisms suspected of being of particular use by terrorist and other criminal organizations.***
- ***Facilitating international information sharing.***
- ***Enhancing outreach and cooperation with the private sector.***

A. Enhancing Law Enforcement Attack on Interagency Basis

A core principle of the *2003 Strategy* is enhancing our ongoing efforts to combat money laundering by ensuring that law enforcement agencies and task forces, including HIFCA, OCDETF, SAR Review Teams and HIDTA Task Forces use and share all available financial databases and analytical tools; focus law enforcement personnel and other resources on high-impact targets and financial systems; and improving Federal government interaction with the financial community.

HIFCAs HIFCAs (currently in New York/New Jersey, San Juan Puerto Rico, Los Angeles, San Francisco, Chicago, Miami, and a Bulk Cash HIFCA along the Southwest Border) have been created specifically to identify and address money laundering in designated geographical areas. HIFCA Task Forces seek to improve the quality of federal money laundering and other financial crime investigations by concentrating the expertise of the participating Federal and state agencies in a unified task force, utilizing all FinCEN, Drug Enforcement Agency (DEA) Special Operations Division, and DHS/ICE Money Laundering Coordination Center financial databases. In addition, FinCEN supplies direct analytical support, either at the HIFCA or from Headquarters. The Departments of the Treasury and Justice continue to review the operation of the HIFCAs in order to enhance their potential and ensure that they complement other appropriate interagency initiatives and task forces, and are preparing a report for the Congress on past operations.

Interagency Narcotics Financing Strategy Center Effectively attacking the financial infrastructure of the most significant drug trafficking organizations requires us to focus, as a primary, not ancillary matter, on the mechanisms and financial systems used to move and launder billions of dollars of illicit funds. As stated in the *2003* Strategy, "the interagency law enforcement community is taking aggressive steps to develop an interagency anti-drug-money laundering financial intelligence center, to serve as a drug-money laundering intelligence and operations center. It is anticipated that this center, currently in the planning stages, will consist of money laundering investigators, prosecutors, and analysts dedicated exclusively to reviewing and acting upon all law enforcement and other financial information in order to develop the highest value targets, identify and disseminate information about developing trends and patterns, and help coordinate financial attacks on the systems, geographic locations, and individuals by and through which drug proceeds are moved and laundered." This effort is ongoing.

Asset Forfeiture We also are continuing our efforts aggressively to utilize asset forfeiture laws and regulations to deprive money launderers and terrorists of their financing infrastructures, as well as all instrumentalities of their crimes. We are succeeding. The Treasury Executive Office for Asset Forfeiture reports that in FY 2003, receipts into the Treasury fund exceeded $250 million. FY 2002 receipts totaled just under $174 million. These are funds and other assets that criminals not only are deprived of, but that can be put to good use either as compensation for victims, or for law enforcement purposes.

Specially Designated Narcotics Traffickers (SDNTs) Program A very potent financial weapon in our war against drug money laundering systems is that wielded by Treasury through the Office of Foreign Assets Control (OFAC). Treasury, through OFAC, in conjunction with the Department of Justice, enforces the IEEPA narcotics trafficking sanctions against Colombian drug cartels under Executive Order 12978. The objectives of the SDNT program are to identify, expose, isolate and incapacitate the businesses and agents of the Colombian drug cartels and to deny them access to the U.S. financial system and to the benefits of trade and transactions involving U.S. businesses and individuals. Targets are identified in consultation with the Drug Enforcement Administration and the narcotics and Dangerous Drug Section of the Department of Justice. Since the inception of the SDNT program in October 1995, some 958 business and individuals have been identified as SDNTs, consisting of 14 Colombian drug "kingpins," 379 businesses and 565 other individuals.

Foreign Narcotics Drug Kingpin Act Program OFAC also administers the Foreign Narcotics Kingpin Designation Act ("Kingpin Act"). The Kingpin Act, enacted in December 1999 operates on a global scale and authorizes the President to deny significant foreign narcotics traffickers, and their related businesses and operatives, access to the U.S. financial system and all trade and transactions involving U.S. companies and individuals these actions when he determines that those foreign narcotics traffickers present a threat to the national security, foreign policy, or economy of the United States. During 2003, the President named 7 new kingpins, including a Colombian narco-terrorist guerilla army, a Colombian narco-terrorist paramilitary force and a Burmese narco-trafficking ethnic guerilla army, bringing the total number designated to 38. Since the inception of the Kingpin Act and after multi-agency consultations, 11 foreign businesses and 15 foreign individuals in Mexico and the Caribbean have been named as derivative ("Tier II") designations by OFAC. These derivative designations are flexible, and permit OFAC to attack the financial infrastructure of these kingpins. This is an ongoing process.

Further, although terrorist financing and drug money laundering differ in some respects, they utilize many of the same financial systems and methods. Two recent cases highlight these connections.

AUC Case On December 4, 2002, federal prosecutors in Houston indicted several individuals, including two high ranking members of Autodefensas Unidas de Colombia (AUC/United Self Defense Forces of Colombia), the Colombian right-wing designated terrorist organization, with drug conspiracy and conspiracy to provide material support or resources to AUC. To date, two of the defendants have pled guilty to the material support § 2339B charge and the drug conspiracy charges. The AUC principals are in Costa Rican custody awaiting extradition.

FARC Case On March 7, 2002, a grand jury in the District of Columbia returned an indictment charging the leader of the 16th front of the Fuerzas Armadas Revolucionarias de Colombia (FARC), and six others, with participating in a drug trafficking conspiracy. Two superseding indictments have added Jorge Briceno-Suarez, the second in command of the FARC and two Peruvian drug traffickers, the Aybar brothers. The Aybar brothers also were indicted in the

Southern District of Florida for providing material support to a terrorist organization by supplying 10,000 AK-47s to the FARC in exchange for cocaine and money.

2. Regulatory Effectiveness

One fact is inescapable--even the most unsophisticated of money laundering and terrorism financing operations likely will intersect the regulated financial system at some point. Pursuant to the *2003 Strategy*, we are taking full advantage of the combination of regulatory and criminal enforcement, including the vital role played by the financial sector, in helping to deter and detect money laundering and terrorist financing. Title III of the USA PATRIOT Act mandates the greatest number of substantial changes to the United States anti-money laundering regulatory regime in recent memory.

Since passage of Title III of the USA PATRIOT Act, Treasury, the Financial Crimes Enforcement Network (FinCEN), the financial regulators, and the Department of Justice have worked together to draft and issue extensive regulations that implement the Act's provisions. Among other things, we have published regulations that --
(i) Permit and facilitate the sharing of critical information between law enforcement and the financial community, as well as among financial institutions themselves;
(ii) Close off our financial borders to foreign shell banks, require additional due diligence for correspondent accounts maintained for foreign financial institutions, and require foreign banks with correspondent accounts in the United States to supply the name of a US agent for service of process as well as the identities of their owners;
(iii) Require US financial institutions to establish customer identification and verification procedures for all new accountholders;
(iv) Expand the universe of financial institutions reporting potentially suspicious activities to FinCEN; and
(v) Expand our basic anti-money laundering regime to include a wide range of financial service providers, such as the securities and futures industry and money services businesses.

Our work is not yet finished. We are working to complete several regulatory packages. First on the list is the issuance of a final regulation that will delineate the scope of the obligation of US financial institutions to conduct due diligence and enhanced due diligence on correspondent accounts maintained for foreign financial institutions and private banking accounts for high net worth foreign individuals. Although the banking, securities, and futures industries have been operating under an interim rule since last year, important questions regarding the application of this statutory provision remain.

We also will complete final regulations requiring other categories of financial institutions, such as those in the insurance and hedge fund industries, to establish anti-money laundering programs. This is an integral component of our anti-money laundering and anti-terrorist financing efforts – to ensure that all available avenues for financial crime are blocked by this basic protection. Similarly, now that we have issued final regulations requiring the banking, securities, futures, and mutual fund industries to establish customer identification programs, we will be drafting regulations applicable to financial institutions in other industries that offer their customers accounts. Finally, we are continuing to explore the appropriate application of the suspicious activity reporting regulations to additional categories of financial institutions. We recently issued a final rule requiring futures commissions merchants to begin reporting in early 2004. We have already proposed to require mutual funds and insurance companies to file such reports as well.

I would like to highlight two of the more significant provisions and how we are implementing them.

USA PATRIOT Act Section 311

A particularly important provision is Section 311 of the Act, which provides the Secretary with the necessary ability to protect the US financial system against specific terrorist financing and money laundering threats posed by foreign financial institutions, accounts, transactions, or even entire jurisdictions. The Secretary can require US financial institutions to take appropriate countermeasures against such threats, countermeasures which include requiring the termination of any correspondent accounts involving the threat. We have utilized this authority in the money laundering context, most recently last month against Burma and two Burmese banks, and we are presently considering its use in connection with the financing of terrorism.

Most importantly, the mere possibility of a Section 311 designation has caused nations to make changes to their legal and regulatory regimes that enhance the global anti-money laundering and anti-terrorist financing infrastructure. That said, however, the Treasury Department will continue to seek out appropriate opportunities to utilize these new powers aggressively, but judiciously, to protect the U.S financial system from corruption by money launderers and terrorist financiers.

USA PATRIOT ACT Section 314a

Additionally, we have created a system pursuant to section 314(a) of the PATRIOT Act to enable law enforcement to locate quickly the accounts and transactions of those suspected of money laundering or the financing of terrorism. While we are still working closely with law enforcement and the financial community on the operation of the system, since its creation, the system has been used to send the names of 256 persons suspected of terrorism financing to financial institutions. This has resulted in 1,739 matches that were passed on to law enforcement.

III. Technology

Just as criminals benefit from enhancements in technology, so must the anti-terrorist financing community. Technology holds one of the keys to our success in the financial war on terrorism. This involves the ability to marshal and synthesize all available information to proactively identify possible instances of the raising, movement and use of illicit funds. More than ever before, we require our financial institutions to produce data and information. Several initiatives should be highlighted. For example, FinCEN is at the first phase of a project involving assistance from the Business Executives for National Security and the Wharton School of the University of Pennsylvania in developing technology that will allow financial institutions to report suspicious transactions more easily and quickly. In addition, as part of an overall plan to enhance our technological platform, FinCEN is developing a new system to manage the Bank Secrecy Act ("BSA") database. "BSA Direct" will involve a significant upgrade to the platform on which the BSA database is maintained, and will provide users with web-based, secure access that allows for faster and easier searching. Finally, we will continue to work to assist financial institutions in developing proactive software to better identify potential terrorist financing activities.

Information developed cannot be applied in a vacuum. Congress recognized that fact when it made enhanced information sharing a central theme of the USA PATRIOT Act. While we have taken substantial steps toward this goal, our challenge remains to find better ways of providing information and feedback. This is not simple. Often the information we develop is highly protected intelligence information that cannot be disclosed, and we are always wary of providing our enemies with a roadmap or a "how-to" guide to manipulating our defenses. That said, we understand the importance of, and are searching for, better ways to share information among ourselves, with the private sector and our global partners.

One example of the use of technology to identify possible sources of terrorist financing is a pilot counterterrorism project undertaken by IRS-CI in Garden City, New York. The Garden City Counterterrorism Lead Development Center is dedicated to providing research and nationwide project support to IRS-CI and the Joint Terrorism Task Force (JTTF) counterterrorism financing investigations. Relying on modern technology, the Center is comprised of a staff of IRS Special Agents, Intelligence Analysts, and civil components from the Service's Tax Exempt/Government Entities Operating Division, who will research leads and field office inquiries concerning terrorism investigations. Center personnel specializing in terrorism issues will develop case knowledge, identify trends, and provide comprehensive data reports to IRS field agents assigned to JTTFs or to those conducting CI counterterrorism financing investigations.

The Center may also serve to de-conflict related investigations among multiple field offices, and will have distinctive analytical capabilities to include link analysis, data matching, and pro-active data modeling. Using data from tax-exempt organizations and other tax-related information that is protected by strict disclosure laws, the Center will analyze information not available to or captured by other law enforcement agencies. Thus, a complete analysis of all financial data will be performed by the Center and disseminated for further investigation. This research, technology, and intuitive modeling, coupled with CI's financial expertise, maximize IRS-CI's impact against sophisticated terrorist organizations.

In conclusion, let me provide you with some sense of how we are using the USA PATRIOT Act powers and enhanced technology, as well as the implementing regulations to combat terrorist financing. Although the process is ongoing, we do have some indication of their effectiveness. For example, as noted earlier, the section 314(a) system has been used in many cases and has resulted in a substantial number of leads. The additional reporting and recordkeeping authorities have enhanced the database FinCEN uses for its research and analysis in supporting terrorism investigations – since September 11th, FinCEN has supported 2,692 terrorism investigations. The Terror Hotline established by FinCEN has resulted in 789 tips passed on to law enforcement. Since the World Trade Center Attacks, FinCEN has made 519 proactive case referrals to law enforcement based upon an analysis of information in the Bank Secrecy Act database. FinCEN also is implementing an Electronic Reports program that will be able to issue these reports in an electronic format, thus enhancing law enforcement's ability better to utilize the information. With the expansion of the suspicious activity reporting regime, financial institutions nationwide have filed 2,842 suspicious activity reports ("SARs") reporting possible terrorist financing. In addition to passing these reports on to law enforcement, FinCEN has and will continue to support these activities.

I will be happy to answer any questions you may have.

-30-

Mr. PUTNAM. Our next witness is George Glass. Mr. Glass has been Director of the Office of Terrorist Finance and Economic Sanctions Policy in the State Department since just after the September 11, 2001, World Trade Center and Pentagon attacks. He presently also serves as Acting Deputy for Energy, Commodities and Sanctions. Prior to September 2001, he was Deputy Chief of Mission at the U.S. Embassy in Bern, Switzerland. He served as U.S. Consul General in Bavaria, Germany, from 1997 to 2002.

Welcome to the subcommittee.

STATEMENT OF GEORGE A. GLASS, DIRECTOR, OFFICE OF TERRORISM FINANCE AND SANCTIONS POLICY, BUREAU OF ECONOMIC AND BUSINESS AFFAIRS, U.S. DEPARTMENT OF STATE

Mr. GLASS. Thank you, Chairman Putnam, Chairman Platts, distinguished members of the committee. I want to thank you for the opportunity to testify today on U.S. efforts to combat terrorist financing.

The United States is engaged in a long-term war against terrorism. I thank you for your support and for providing the necessary tools for waging this war. This fight requires actions on multiple fronts.

We have made substantial progress, but an awful lot remains to be done. Since September 11, 2001, the United States, as noted, has ordered the freezing in the United States of the assets of 344 individuals and entities linked to terrorism.

We have supported the submission by dozens of countries around the world of some 244 al-Qaeda-linked names for inclusion in the U.N. asset freeze list requiring all countries around the world to take action against these names. We have frozen approximately $136.8 million in almost 50 countries, including the United States. We have instructed our embassies formally to approach every country, every government around the world some 75 times to freeze each name that we designate.

We have developed a broad international coalition against terrorist finance. We have stopped a major hawala network based out of Somalia, which had been operating in some 40 countries. We acted against supporters of the Asian terrorist group linked to the Bali disco bombing. We designated charities funding Hamas, and we disrupted Saudi terrorist financiers.

We assisted the strengthening of national laws, regulations and regulatory institutions around the world to better combat terrorist finance and money laundering, and through all of this we made it harder for terrorists and for their supporters to use financial systems.

Particularly important in making this happen is the fact that we have come a very long way over the past 2 years in terms of U.S. Government interagency coordination. We improved the degree to which all agencies with equities related to the pursuit of terrorist financing cooperate and coordinate their efforts. This strong interagency teamwork involves the intelligence and law enforcement communities as well as State, Treasury, Homeland Security, Justice, and the financial regulatory agencies all collectively pursuing understanding of the system of financial backers, facilitators and intermediaries that play a role in this shadowy financial world.

A key weapon against terrorist finance has been the President's Executive Order 13224, signed on September 23, 2001, just 12 days after the terrorist attacks of September 11th. The order provided the basic structure and authorities for an effort unprecedented in history to identify and freeze the assets of individuals and entities associated with terrorism across the board. Under the Executive Order the administration has frozen the assets of 344 individuals and entities on 47 separate occasions. The agencies cooperating in this effort are in daily contact, looking at and evaluating new names and targets for possible asset freeze.

However, our scope is not just limited to freezing assets. We have very successfully used other actions as well, including developing diplomatic initiatives with other governments to conduct audits and investigations, exchanging information on records, cooperating in law enforcement and intelligence efforts, and in shaping new regulatory initiatives.

We also have a very substantial interagency commitment that provides counterterrorist finance training to help our coalition partners develop and enhance their capabilities to detect, disrupt and dismantle terrorist financing networks by strengthening the legal frameworks, providing financial investigative training, training banking regulatory communities on suspicious transactions, developing financial intelligence units that cooperate internationally, and strengthening the ability of prosecutors to bring terrorist financiers to justice. We have already assessed and are providing assistance to a number of high priority countries in this area.

Internationally, the U.N.'s role in response to the challenge of terrorist financing has been significant. This is extremely important because most of the assets making their way to terrorists are not under U.S. control; and, when it comes to al-Qaeda in particular, it means that when an individual or entity is included in the U.N. sanctions list, all 191 U.N. member states are obligated to implement the sanctions, including asset freezes against these individuals and entities. The U.N. has added a total of some 244 al-Qaeda-linked names to its consolidated list since September 11th.

U.S. efforts against terrorist finance are active in all regions of the world. Saudi Arabia has been one important focus. On October 12, 2001, we froze the assets of Saudi millionaire Yasin al Kadi because of his links to al-Qaeda. He was designated and listed by the U.N. for worldwide sanctions. Subsequently we and the Saudi Government submitted, on March 11, 2002, the names of the Somali and Bosnian branches of the charity al Haramain to the United Nations, also for worldwide asset freezing. We and the Saudis also submitted the name of Wael Julaidan, a prominent Saudi al-Qaeda financier, to the U.N. for sanctions, including asset freeze, on September 6, 2002.

Saudi Arabia has made changes to its banking and charity systems to help strangle the funds that keep al-Qaeda in business.

Another key focus of terrorist finance has been Hamas, which was first formally designated by the U.S. Government as a foreign terrorist organization in October 1997. On August 22nd of this year, just a few months ago, the President announced the designation for asset freezing of five key Hamas fundraisers. On that day he also announced the designation of six top Hamas leaders. Hamas's suicide bombings demonstrate the organization's commitment to undermining any real efforts to move toward permanent peace between Israel and the Palestinians. Shutting off the flow of funds to Hamas is crucial to reducing Hamas's ability to carry out its activities and to thwart progress toward peace.

In Asia we have also been active. We have been working closely with the governments in Asia to stop funding for Jemaah Islamiyah, an organization linked to the September 2002 Bali disco bombing.

Another key focus has been hawalas, or informal money remittance systems, which have posed special challenges in the Middle East and South Asia. We have made a special effort to engage countries on hawalas and other informal networks, encouraging innovative solutions, including via technical assistance and regulatory oversight.

Mr. Chairman, asset freezes and arrests get the headlines, but diplomatic action also makes a difference. When we talk about diplomatic approaches for dealing with targets, we are talking about getting other governments to cooperate in the war against terrorist financing by taking concrete actions of their own, including law enforcement and intelligence actions, as well as getting them to speak out publicly against terrorist groups.

It has involved encouraging foreign governments to prosecute key terrorists and terrorist financiers, to extradite a terrorist financier, to pass strong antiterrorist financing legislation, to prohibit funds from being sent to a charity, and to make sure companies funneling funds to terrorists are shut down.

We have made it more difficult for terrorists to move and collect funds, but we still have a long way to go given the dimensions of this challenge.

Mr. Chairman, I would like to thank you both for the opportunity to address this important issue.

Mr. PUTNAM. Thank you, Mr. Glass.

[The prepared statement of Mr. Glass follows:]

TESTIMONY OF GEORGE GLASS
DIRECTOR OF THE OFFICE OF TERRORISM FINANCE
AND SANCTIONS POLICY
DEPARTMENT OF STATE
TO THE HOUSE COMMITTEE ON GOVERNMENT REFORM'S
SUBCOMMITTEE ON TECHNOLOGY AND INFORMATION POLICY,
INTERGOVERNMENTAL RELATIONS AND THE CENSUS
December 15, 2003

U.S. INTERAGENCY EFFORTS TO COMBAT TERRORIST FINANCING

Mr. Chairman and distinguished members of the Committee: thank you for the opportunity to testify on U.S. efforts to combat terrorist financing.

The United States is engaged in a long-term war against terrorism. I thank you for your support and for providing the necessary tools for waging this war. This fight requires actions on multiple fronts. A critical front is the effort to defeat, disrupt, and destroy the financial networks that sustain terrorists and finance their operations. We have made substantial progress, but a lot remains to be done. Since September 11, 2001, the U.S. has:

-- ordered the freezing in the U.S. of the assets of 344 individuals and entities linked to terrorism;

-- supported the submission by dozens of countries around the world of 244 Al-Qaida-linked names for inclusion in the UN asset-freeze list, requiring all countries to act against these names;

-- frozen approximately $136.8 million in almost 50 countries, including the U.S.;

-- instructed our embassies formally to approach every government around the world some 75 times to freeze each name we designate;

-- developed a broad international coalition against terrorist finance;

-- stopped a major *hawala* network based out of Somalia; acted against supporters of the Asian terrorist group linked to the Bali disco bombing; designated charities funding Hamas; disrupted Saudi terrorist financiers;

-- assisted the strengthening of national laws, regulations and regulatory institutions around the world to better combat terrorist finance and money laundering;

-- and made it harder for terrorists and their supporters to use financial systems.

Particularly important in making this happen is the fact that we have come a very long way over the past two years in terms of USG interagency coordination. We improved the degree to which all U.S. agencies with equities related to the pursuit of terrorist financing cooperate and coordinate their efforts. This strong interagency teamwork involves the intelligence and law enforcement communities, as well as State, Treasury, Homeland Security, Justice and the financial regulatory agencies, collectively pursuing an understanding of the system of financial backers, facilitators and intermediaries that play a role in this shadowy financial world. It involves the Treasury Department, coordinating the policy process by which we examine actions to disrupt these financial networks. It involves the Department of Justice leading the investigations and prosecutions in a seamless, coordinated campaign against terrorist sources of financing. And, it involves the State Department leading the interagency process through which we develop and sustain the bilateral and multilateral relationships, strategies and activities, including -- in coordination with Justice, Treasury, Homeland Security and the financial regulatory agencies -- the provision of training and technical assistance, to win vital international support for and cooperation with our efforts. Many of these international efforts are outlined in the recently published *National Money Laundering Strategy*. Our task has been to identify, track and pursue terrorist financing targets and to work with the international community to take measures to thwart the ability of terrorists to raise and channel the funds they need to survive and carry out their horrible acts.

A key weapon in this effort has been the President's Executive Order 13224, which was signed on September 23, 2001, just 12 days after the terrorist attacks of September 11. That Order provided the basic structure and authorities for an effort, unprecedented in history, to identify and freeze the assets of individuals and entities associated with terrorism across the board. Under that Executive Order, the Administration has frozen the assets of 344 individuals and entities on 47 separate occasions. The agencies cooperating in this effort are in daily contact, looking at and evaluating new names and targets for possible asset freeze. However, our scope is not just limited to freezing assets.

Under a 1996 law, the State Department has continued to publicly designate and re-designate major foreign terrorist groups as Foreign Terrorist Organizations (FTOs). The Secretary of State's formal designations, made in consultation with the Attorney General and Secretary of Treasury, freeze assets in the U.S. of the designated group, make it a criminal offense to knowingly provide funds or other forms of material support to the designated groups, and deny visas to members and leaders of the designated organization in the U.S. Currently 36 groups are formally designated.

We have very successfully used other actions as well, including developing diplomatic initiatives with other governments to conduct audits and investigations, exchanging information on records, cooperating in law enforcement and intelligence efforts, and in shaping new regulatory initiatives.

We recognize, however, that designating names -- along with arrests -- is the action that is most publicly visible. But, designations are, in no way, the only regulatory action underway. Every approach the interagency Policy Coordination Committee has adopted regarding a specific target has involved extensive, careful work. We need to make sure we have credible information that provides a reasonable basis linking the individual or entity to terrorism; we need to weigh the options available to us for addressing the target; we need to identify the most effective approach, realizing that we may shift gears and adopt a different strategy later on. We want to be right, legal and effective. In some cases we support public action, such as designations, in other cases we choose other methods, including law enforcement, intelligence, or getting another country to undertake law enforcement or intelligence action.

We also have a substantial interagency commitment that provides counter-terrorist finance training to help our coalition partners develop and/or enhance their capabilities to detect, disrupt and dismantle terrorist financing networks by strengthening the legal frameworks, providing financial investigative training, training the banking regulatory communities on suspicious transactions, developing financial intelligence units that cooperate internationally, and strengthening the ability of prosecutors to bring terrorist financiers to justice. The Departments of State, Treasury and Justice established an interagency Terrorist Financing Working Group (TFWG), chaired by the State Department, to coordinate government efforts to identify, prioritize and assess those countries vulnerable to terrorist exploitation. Groups of experts, including DOJ money laundering prosecutors, interagency law enforcement and regulatory members, have provided extensive on-the-ground assessments of such countries' vulnerabilities in an effort to develop and provide targeted training and technical assistance to those countries identified as most vulnerable. We have already assessed and are providing assistance to a number of priority countries. Resources permitting, we shall expand this effort. At the end of the day, all our actions combined, and the efforts of countries around the world, have succeeded in making it more difficult for terrorists to collect and move funds around the world, in particular through formal banking channels.

Internationally, the UN's role in responding to the challenge of terrorist financing has been significant: The UN, through UN Security Council Resolutions 1373, 1267, 1333, 1390 and 1455 helped give international impetus and legitimacy to asset freezes and to underscore the global commitment against terrorist financing. This is extremely important, because: (1) most of the assets making their way to terrorists are not under U.S. control; and (2) when it comes to al Qaida in particular, it means that when an individual or entity is included on the UN's sanctions list, all 191 UN Member States are obligated to implement the sanctions, including asset freezes against these individuals and entities. It has added a total of some 244 al Qaida-linked names to its consolidated list since September 11.

Another very important actor in international efforts to combat terrorist financing has been the Financial Action Task Force (FATF), a multilateral organization of 33 members individually and collectively devoted to combating money laundering. FATF has adopted 40 recommendations on the elimination of money laundering and an additional, complementary eight special recommendations on combating terrorist finance. FATF is monitoring compliance with its recommendations in coordination with regional bodies, the UN Counter-Terrorism Committee (CTC), and the G-8-initiated Counter-terrorism

Action Group (CTAG). FATF is planning assessments of country-needs for technical assistance to improve local ability to combat terrorist financing. It is in large part due to FATF's focus and efforts on terrorist financing, for instance, that the Indonesian Parliament passed important amendments to its anti-money laundering law on September 16, amendments that will improve the country's ability to take actions against terrorist financing. Similarly, FATF's efforts led the Philippines to pass legislation in March that will significantly increase that country's ability to carry out meaningful anti-terrorist financing measures. A FATF team has worked with the Saudi government to review new regulations as well as pending legislation. FATF advises on whether such regulations and legislation meet international standards of effective instruments to combat money-laundering and terrorist financing.

In November 2003, the Group of Experts to Control Money Laundering of the Organization of American States' Inter-American Drug Abuse Control Commission (OAS/CICAD), during a session chaired by the Department of Justice, finalized model provisions to guide legislators in adopting criminal offenses for terrorist financing, mechanisms to immediately block terrorist assets in accordance with United Nations Security Council resolutions, and to control alternative remittance systems, such as *Hawala* methods that have been used to finance terrorism. The OAS Inter-American Committee Against Terrorism (CICTE) is planning training for prosecutors and judges in member countries on terrorism and terrorist financing.

U.S. efforts against terrorist finance are active in all regions of the world. Saudi Arabia has been one important focus. On October 12, 2001, we froze the assets of Saudi millionaire Yasin al Kadi because of his links to al Qaida, and he was designated and listed by the UN for world-wide sanctions. Subsequently, we and the Saudi government submitted on March 11, 2002, the names of the Somali and Bosnian branches of the charity al Haramain to the UN also for worldwide asset-freezing. We and the Saudis also submitted the name of Wael Julaidan, a prominent Saudi al Qaida financier, to the UN for sanctions, including asset freeze, on September 6, 2002. The Saudis have frozen substantial assets. These are a few examples of actions that have been publicly visible.

In January of this year, we launched a senior-level dialogue designed to improve communications between the U.S. and Saudi Arabia on terrorist financing issues. As a result of the May 12, 2003 bombings in Saudi Arabia that left 34 dead, including 8 Americans, the dialogue has intensified.

Saudi Arabia has made some changes to its banking and charity systems to help strangle the funds that keep al-Qaida in business. As part of a State-led interagency assistance program, Federal Banking Regulators have provided specialized anti-money laundering and counter terrorist financing training to their Saudi counter-parts. Saudi Arabia's new banking regulations place strict controls on accounts held by charities. Charities cannot deposit or withdraw cash from their bank accounts. And Saudi Arabia has banned the collection of donations at mosques and instructed retail establishments to remove charity collection boxes from their premises. This is undoubtedly challenging for Saudi Arabia, but the Saudi Government has undertaken these measures because it understands that terrorists are more likely to use such funds than those channeled through formal banking channels. Saudi Arabia is working with us closely in the context of the new task force on terrorist financing. As part of the State-led interagency Terrorist Finance Working Group (TFWG), experts from the FBI and IRS have completed the first part of a training course designed to strengthen the financial investigative capabilities of the Saudi security forces, with more advanced courses to follow. Having said all this, I want to stress that this is a work in progress. We have reason to believe that the new task force on terrorist financing will be effective but we will need to see results. We believe the Saudi Government is implementing its new charity regulations, but there too, we will need to see results.

Another key focus of terrorist finance effort has been HAMAS, which was first formally designated by the USG as a Foreign Terrorist organization in October, 1997 and has been re-designated every two years since. On August 22 of this year, the President announced the designation for asset-freezing of the following five HAMAS fundraisers: CBSP *(Comite de Bienfaisance et de Secours aux Palestiniens),* ASP *(Association de Secours Palestinien), Interpal,* Palestinian Association in Austria *(PVOE)* and Sanabil Association for Relief and Development. He also announced the designation of six top HAMAS leaders *(Sheikh Yassin, Imad al Alami, Usama Hamdan, Khalid Mishaal, Musa Abu Marzouk and Abdel Aziz Rantisi).* Earlier this year, the U.S. also designated for asset-freezing another HAMAS charity operating in various parts of Europe, the al Aqsa Foundation.

HAMAS' suicide bombings demonstrate the organization's commitment to undermining any real efforts to move towards a permanent peace between Israel and the Palestinians. Shutting off the flow of funds to HAMAS is crucial to reducing HAMAS' ability to carry out its activities and to thwart progress towards peace. HAMAS is also clearly a threat to Palestinian reform, including Palestinians committed to a negotiated peace. HAMAS has used its charities to strengthen its own standing among Palestinians and recruit supporters at the expense of the Palestinian Authority.

In light of this, the U.S. welcomed the EU's decision in September to designate HAMAS in its entirety as a terrorist organization. Previously, the EU had only designated Izzadin al Kassem, HAMAS' "military wing" as a terrorist entity.

We have also urged governments throughout the region to take steps to shut down both HAMAS operations and offices, and to do everything possible to disrupt the flow of funding to HAMAS, and other Palestinian organizations that have engaged in terror to disrupt peace efforts. Although some of these financial flows may be used to support charitable activities, which aids recruitment of supporters, some of this money frees up funds used to support HAMAS' rejectionist and terrorist activities. We will continue to engage with regional governments to prevent all funding of HAMAS and other groups that have engaged in terror.

Also worth noting are actions taken elsewhere in the Middle East. The United Arab Emirates, Bahrain, Egypt and Qatar have also passed anti-money laundering legislation and all Gulf Cooperation Council member states have increased oversight of their banking systems. Kuwait, Saudi Arabia, Bahrain, Qatar and Oman are devising ways to prevent the misuse and abuse of charities for terrorist purposes.

In Asia, we have worked closely with governments to stop funding for Jemaah Islamiyah (JI), an organization linked to the September 2002 Bali disco bombing. On October 23, 2002 fifty countries petitioned the UN to designate this al Qaida-linked organization. Since then, the international community has acted to add the names of 22 key individuals from this organization to the UN (and US) asset-freeze list.

Hawalas, or informal money remittance systems, have posed special challenges in the Middle East and South Asia. These systems operate around the world, often beyond the purview of bank regulators. They have existed for thousands of years and are not necessarily illegal undertakings, but are susceptible to misuse. We have made a special effort to engage countries on *Hawalas* and other informal networks, encouraging innovative solutions, including via technical assistance and regulatory oversight. In April 2002 the United Arab Emirates hosted a major international conference to make countries aware of how *Hawalas* operate and steps that might be taken to ensure they are not used to support terrorism. The EU last month hosted another internal meeting on *Hawalas*. Follow-up continues wherever *Hawalas* are common by U.S. and internationally sponsored technical assistance and training teams.

Asset-freezes and arrests get the headlines, but "diplomatic action" also makes a difference in the world of terrorist finance. Let me just briefly characterize for you the forceful types of actions that we refer to under the rubric "diplomatic action," a phrase that we well know isn't always assumed to be a synonym for "armed and dangerous." When we talk about diplomatic approaches for dealing with targets, we are talking about getting other governments to cooperate in the war against terrorist financing by taking concrete actions of their own, including law enforcement and intelligence actions, as well as getting them to speak out publicly against terrorist groups. It has involved encouraging foreign governments to prosecute key terrorists and terrorist financiers; to extradite a terrorist financier; to pass strong anti-terrorist financing legislation; to prohibit funds from being sent to a charity; and to make sure companies funneling funds to terrorists are shut down. Diplomatic action also means improving conditions for our colleagues in other agencies to work more effectively with their foreign counterparts in the fight against terrorist financing. The results obtained through such diplomatic strategies are crucial to our long-term success.

As we move forward with refined strategies, we will continue to work actively with other governments in different regions of the world to make further progress in our fight against terrorist financing. In Saudi Arabia, we will continue our cooperation to achieve actions such as the joint submission to the UN for asset freezing of the Bosnian and Somali branches of the Saudi charity al Haramain, and the similar designation of Wael Julaydan, a prominent Saudi al Qaida financier. These actions as well as other important initiatives such as cooperation in building a joint task force on terrorist financing, we believe are, and will continue to be, productive and in the interest of protecting and saving American lives. In Asia, we will continue to work with governments to confront JI, including its sources of funding. Three months ago the UN listed twenty new names of individuals associated with JI whose assets UN member states are obligated to freeze. In this hemisphere, as mentioned above, the OAS/CICAD Money Laundering Experts Group is drafting model laws and regulations that nations may adapt, enact, and implement to fulfill their FATF commitment to combat terrorist financing. We continue to identify vulnerabilities around the world and to work with other countries to address them effectively. Our capacity-building and technical assistance is vital in this effort. We have made it more difficult for terrorists to move and collect funds, but we still have a long way to go given the dimensions of this challenge.

Mr. Chairman, thank you for the opportunity to address this important issue.

Drafted: EB/ESP:NRothstein 76203

cleared:
EB/ESP:GGlass ok
D:KReider ok
E:JDuncan (info)
P:AGordon ok
H:JLande ok
H:ASiebert (info)
S/CT:TNavratil (info)
S/CT:Rstapleton ok
S/CT: GNovis ok
EAP/IMBS:EReddick ok
EAP/RSP:CCohen ok
EUR.ERA:FParker ok
EUR/PGI:LReasor ok
INL:ERindler ok
IO/PHO:APerez ok
NEA/RA:PSutphin
NEA/ARP:PHeffernan ok
S/CT:MMiller ok
S/CT:Mkraft ok

Mr. PUTNAM. Our next witness is Mr. Carl Whitehead, Special Agent in Charge here in Tampa, Mr. Whitehead with the FBI. Mr. Whitehead entered duty with the FBI in 1982 and has served in the Detroit, Los Angeles, New Orleans and San Antonio field offices.

During his career Mr. Whitehead has directed several significant drug, public corruption, and violent crimes investigations, most recently as an inspector in the Inspection Division with FBI headquarters in Washington. Mr. Whitehead has significantly contributed to ensuring the operational and administrative efficiencies of the FBI.

Welcome, Mr. Whitehead. You are recognized.

STATEMENT OF CARL WHITEHEAD, SPECIAL AGENT IN CHARGE, TAMPA OFFICE, FEDERAL BUREAU OF INVESTIGATION, U.S. DEPARTMENT OF JUSTICE, ACCOMPANIED BY FRANK J. FABIAN, UNIT CHIEF, TERRORIST FINANCING OPERATIONS SECTION, WASHINGTON, DC

Mr. WHITEHEAD. Thank you. Good morning, Mr. Chairmen and members of both subcommittees. I would like to, on behalf of the FBI, to thank you for giving us the opportunity to participate in this forum and to provide comments on the FBI achievements, together with our partners, in the ongoing effort to identify, dismantle, and disrupt sources of terrorist financing. I also appreciate the opportunity to highlight the FBI's use of information technology to better identify and isolate suspicious transactions related to terrorist financing.

As you are aware, since September 11, 2001, the FBI has relocated or reallocated substantial resources to protect the American people from another terrorist attack. At FBI headquarters, the Counterterrorism Division has been reorganized to provide a more centralized, comprehensive, and proactive approach to investigating terrorist-related matters. In the field we have increased the number of agents devoted to terrorism cases and expanded the ranks of our Joint Terrorism Task Forces [JTTFs], which involve agents and officers from a host of State, local and Federal partners.

Given the focus of this hearing, you clearly appreciate that the fight against terrorist financing is a major front in our war on terror. Simply put, terrorists and their networks require funding in some form to exist and operate. Whether the funding and financial support is minimal or substantial, it leaves a financial trail that can be traced, tracked and exploited for proactive and reactive purposes.

Being able to identify and track financial transactions and links after a terrorist act has occurred is only a small part of the mission for us. The key is honing our ability to exploit financial information to identify previously unknown terrorist cells, recognize potential terrorist activity, and predict and prevent potential terrorist acts.

To this end the FBI has bolstered its ability to effectively combat terrorism through the formation of the Terrorist Financing Operations Section [TFOS]. TFOS was created to combine the FBI's traditional expertise in conducting complex criminal financial investigations with advanced technologies and the powerful legislative tools provided by the U.S. Patriot Act. To achieve its goals TFOS has developed a strong support network within the private financial sector and encouraged the cooperation and coordination among law enforcement and intelligence agencies both here and abroad.

In the past several months, TFOS has demonstrated its capabilities by conducting near real-time financial tracking of a terrorist cell and providing specific and identifiable information to a foreign intelligence agency, which resulted in the prevention of six potentially deadly terrorist attacks.

This recent success is not an isolated one. The FBI has engaged in extensive coordination with the authorities of numerous foreign governments in terrorist financing matters, leading to joint investigative efforts throughout the world. These joint investigations have successfully targeted the financing of several overseas al-Qaeda cells. Additionally, with the assistance of relations established with the central banks of several strategic countries, successful disruptions of al-Qaeda financing have been accomplished in countries such as UAE, Pakistan, Afghanistan, and Indonesia.

Those of us in the field have also benefited from the increased coordination and liaison being spearheaded at the national-international level. TFOS has provided operational support to FBI field divisions across the United States. This assistance is providing a form of financial analytical support, major case management, financial link analysis, and the deployment of teams of experts to develop investigative plans to analyze large volumes of documents and data. TFOS has provided this type of operational support in the al-Qaeda sleeper cell cases in Buffalo and Portland and many others.

Here in Tampa, we have seen the results of increased coordination and cooperation in investigations like the criminal case against Sami al-Arian, the alleged U.S. leader of the Palestinian Islamic Jihad, and the World Islamic Study Enterprise. As has been widely reported, that case resulted in the closure of several front companies suspected of funneling money to support PIJ operations against Israel.

In August 2002, an investigation led to the deportation of Mazen Al-Najjar, the brother-in-law of Sami al-Arian and a known PIJ member.

In February, following a 50-count indictment for RICO and material support of terrorism violations, the FBI arrested al-Arian and three other U.S.-based members of the PIJ. The FBI also executed over 11 search warrants associated with this case.

Despite the success and other achievements outlined in my written testimony, we cannot rest in our efforts to combat terrorist financing. The FBI has an ability to not only react, but proactively and strategically think about potential threats and future case developments. Technology is an important tool in this effort.

The Proactive Exploits Group within TFOS has conducted an extensive review of data-mining software and link analysis tools currently utilized by other government entities and private industries to assess their potential use by the FBI. The Proactive Exploits Group has already created an interactive computer playbook generator that can assist investigators in determining data sources to be queried in their cases, depending on the quantity and quality of their investigative data.

Working with outside experts, the FBI has also developed a process by where the Financial Intelligence Analysis Unit within TFOS can batch query multiple data bases for potential, after matches by names, telephone numbers, e-mails, etc. This batch process has the potential to save the FBI hundreds if not thousands of hours of data input and query time on each occasion it is used. It also facilitates rapid acquisition and the sharing of information with other agencies.

In my submitted remarks, several ongoing data analysis projects are outlined in more detail. It is important to understand, however, that these projects and similar initiatives by TFOS seek only to more fully exploit information already obtained by the FBI in the course of its investigations, or through appropriate legal process, and where there is an articulated law enforcement need. The FBI does not seek to access personal or financial information outside of these constraints.

I would like to use my final moments with the committee to underscore the FBI's commitment to greater coordination and cooperation with other agencies in this fight against terrorism. At a national level, TFOS routinely participates in joint endeavors with the agencies presented here today. We are an active participant on the Policy Coordinating Committee on Terrorist Financing, which is chaired by the Treasury Department, and focuses on ensuring that all relevant components of the Federal Government are acting in a coordinated and effective manner to combat terrorism financing.

We have also benefited from agreements between the Department of Homeland Security and DOJ that clarify our complementary missions in the terrorist financing and money laundering arenas. At a local level, we have long appreciated the fact that the most difficult cases must be tackled in concert with our sister agencies. That reality has become all the more clear as we face the challenges of a terrorist threat. Terrorism is a global problem that reaches into every community. A solution is a willingness to engage in unprecedented national and international cooperation and an openness to new tools and new ways of thinking. The FBI is committed to both.

Again I offer my gratitude and appreciation to you, Chairman Putnam and Chairman Platts, as well as the distinguished members of both committees for dedicating your time and effort to this important issue.

Mr. PUTNAM. Thank you, Mr. Whitehead.

[The prepared statement of Mr. Whitehead follows:]

CARL WHITEHEAD
SPECIAL AGENT IN CHARGE,
TAMPA DIVISION
FEDERAL BUREAU OF INVESTIGATION
Before the
HOUSE COMMITTEE ON GOVERNMENT REFORM
SUBCOMMITTEE ON GOVERNMENT EFFICIENCY and FINANCIAL MANAGEMENT and SUBCOMMITTEE ON TECHNOLOGY and INFORMATION POLICY and the CENSUS

December 15, 2003

Good morning Mr. Chairmen and members of both the Subcommittee on Government Efficiency and Financial Management and the Subcommittee on Technology and Information Policy and the Census. On behalf of the Federal Bureau of Investigation (FBI), I would like to express my gratitude to both Subcommittees for affording us the opportunity to participate in this forum and to provide comments on the FBI's achievements, together with our partners in the war on terror, in the effort to identify, dismantle and disrupt sources of terrorist financing. I also appreciate the opportunity to highlight the FBI's use of information technology to better identify and isolate suspicious transactions related to terrorist financing, as well as the continuing enhancement of interagency cooperation in the battle against terrorist financing.

Since September 11, 2001, the FBI has reallocated substantial resources to protect the American people from another terrorist attack. The FBI's Counterterrorism Division has been reorganized to provide a more centralized, comprehensive and proactive approach to investigating terrorism-related matters to effectively disrupt and dismantle terrorist organizations before they are able to conduct attacks against citizens of the United States. And, given the changing nature of terrorism and the pace of technological innovations, the FBI has consistently been called upon to devise and implement new methods and techniques to identify, prosecute and, most importantly, prevent future crimes and attacks.

The fight against terrorist financing is a major front in our war on terror. We recognize that terrorists, their networks and support structures require funding in some form to exist and operate. Whether the funding and financial support is minimal or substantial, it leaves a financial trail that can be traced, tracked, and exploited for proactive and reactive purposes. Being able to identify and track financial transactions and links *after* a terrorist act has occurred or a terrorist activity has been identified is only a small part of the mission; the key lies in exploiting financial information to identify previously unknown terrorist cells, recognize potential terrorist activity or planning, and predict and prevent potential terrorist acts. To this end, the FBI has bolstered its ability to effectively combat terrorism through the formation of the Terrorist Financing Operations Section (TFOS).

TFOS was created to combine the FBI's traditional expertise in conducting complex criminal financial investigations with advanced technologies and the powerful legislative tools provided in the USA PATRIOT Act. TFOS has built upon these established mechanisms by developing a strong support network within the private financial sector, as well as furthering cooperation and coordination among law enforcement and intelligence agencies, both domestic and foreign, to form the preeminent terrorist financing investigative operation. In the past several months, TFOS has demonstrated its capabilities by conducting near real-time financial tracking of a terrorist cell and providing specific and identifiable information to a foreign intelligence agency, which resulted in the prevention of six, potential deadly terrorist attacks.

The TFOS mission includes: conducting full financial analysis of terrorist suspects and their financial support structures in the US and abroad; coordinating joint participation, liaison, and outreach efforts to exploit financial resources of private, government, and foreign entities; utilizing FBI and Legal Attaché expertise and relationships to fully develop financial information from foreign law enforcement and private agencies, including the deployment of TFOS personnel abroad; working jointly with the intelligence community to fully exploit intelligence information to further terrorist investigations; working jointly with the law enforcement and regulatory communities; developing predictive models and conducting data analysis to facilitate the identification of previously unknown or "sleeper" terrorist suspects; and providing the financial component to classified counterterrorism investigations in support of the FBI's counterterrorism responsibilities.

1. <u>Achievements towards the identification, dismantlement and disruption of sources of terrorist financing:</u>

Before addressing some specific, investigative accomplishments in the fight against terrorist financing since 9/11/01, it is important to mention our progress in broad areas. For instance, international awareness and cooperation on the problem of terrorist financing has reached unparalleled levels. Outreach with, and cooperation from, the private sector has been outstanding and continues to develop--particularly the level of two-way interaction between law enforcement and the private sector. The resulting ability to access and obtain information in a timely fashion has significantly enhanced the FBI's ability to identify, investigate, and resolve immediate threat situations involving potential terrorist activity. Moreover, the ability to conduct near real-time monitoring of specifically identified financial activity has been invaluable not only to investigations ongoing in the US, but to foreign law enforcement and intelligence agencies in related investigations.

As an example of our liaison and outreach efforts, extensive training and support of international investigations by TFOS has resulted in Agent visits, exchanges and training programs involving countries in Europe, Southeast Asia, the Middle East and South America. In support of specific high profile joint terrorist financial investigative matters, a number of countries and agencies, including the United Kingdom, Switzerland, Canada and Europol, have detailed investigators to TFOS on a temporary duty basis. TFOS has engaged in extensive coordination with authorities of numerous foreign governments in terrorist financing matters, leading to joint investigative efforts throughout the world. These joint investigations have successfully targeted the financing of several overseas al-Qa'ida cells. Furthermore, with the assistance of relationships established with the central banks of several strategic countries, successful disruptions of al-Qa'ida financing have been accomplished in counties such as the UAE, Pakistan, Afghanistan, and Indonesia.

As part of its outreach effort, TFOS has developed a specific terrorist financing and money laundering crimes curriculum for international training that includes topics such as: acquiring and handling evidence in document intensive financial investigations, major case management techniques, forensic examination tools, and methods of terrorist financing. At the request of the US Department of State, TFOS has led an interagency team to provide this curriculum to a number of countries (and is scheduled to provide it to approximately 38 countries) identified as needing law enforcement training on conducting terrorist financing investigations.

Needless to say, access to foreign banking records is often critical to effectively following the money. Through these training and outreach initiatives, TFOS has been able to obtain direct access to records provided by foreign central banks in numerous countries. In return, TFOS has also been able to assist these and other countries with the reciprocal sharing of financial information.

TFOS has cultivated and maintains a contact database of private industry and government sources and persons who can provide financial data, including near real-time monitoring of financial transactions. Many of these contacts can be reached or accessed on a 24 hour/7 days a week basis, allowing TFOS to respond rapidly to critical incidents.

Through these contacts and with appropriate legal process, TFOS has access to data and information from a variety of entities including: Banking Institutions, the Credit/Debit Card Sector, Money Services Businesses, the Securities/Brokerages Sector, Insurance Companies, Travel Agencies, Internet Service Providers, the Telecommunications Industry, Law Enforcement, State/Federal Regulatory Agencies, Public and Open Source Data Providers, the Intelligence Community, and International Law Enforcement and Intelligence Contacts. The timeliness and accessibility of the data from these sources is contingent on a variety of factors, including whether the acquisition of the information requires legal process, the search capabilities of the data provider, and the size and depth of the data request. Nevertheless, as I've noted, the ability to access and obtain this type of information in a time sensitive and urgent manner has significantly enhanced the FBI's ability to identify, investigate and resolve immediate threat situations involving potential terrorist activity.

In addition to these developments, the FBI, working in coordination with other entities of the US government, has participated in the following successes pertaining to terrorist financing:

1 An FBI Joint Terrorism Task Force in Charlotte, North Carolina, utilized racketeering statutes to obtain criminal convictions and, thus, disrupt and dismantle a Hizballah procurement and fundraising cell. Twenty-six individuals were arrested for crimes including immigration fraud, visa fraud, cigarette smuggling, interstate transportation of stolen property, fraud, bank fraud, bribery, money laundering, racketeering, and providing material support to a terrorist organization.

•

2 The FBI coordinated with the Treasury Department's Office of Foreign Asset Control (OFAC) to justify the blocking of Holy Land Foundation for Relief and Development (HLF) assets and the closing of its US offices, shutting down Hamas' largest fund-

raising entity in the US. The HLF had been linked to the funding of Hamas terrorist activities, and in 2000, raised $13 million.

•

3 Offices of the Benevolence International Foundation (BIF), a US based charity, were shut down and its assets and records blocked following an OFAC and FBI investigation which determined the charity was being used to funnel money to al Qa'ida. In February 2003, Enaam Arnaout, the head of BIF, pleaded guilty to racketeering conspiracy, admitting he fraudulently obtained charitable donations in order to provide financial assistance to persons engaged in violent activities overseas.

•

4 A criminal case against Sami Al Arian, the alleged US leader of the Palestinian Islamic Jihad (PIJ), and the World Islamic Studies Enterprise forced the closure of several front companies suspected of funneling money to support PIJ operations against Israel. In August 2002, the investigation led to the deportation of Mazen Al-Najjar, the brother-in-law of Sami Al Arian and a known PIJ member. In February, following a 50-count indictment for RICO and Material Support of Terrorism violations, the FBI arrested Al-Arian and three other US-based members of the Palestinian Islamic Jihad, including Sameeh Hammoudeh, Hatim Naji Fariz, and Ghassan Ballout. The FBI also executed seven search warrants associated with this action.

•

5 TFOS has provided operational support to FBI Field Divisions across the United States to enhance their intelligence/criminal investigations of individuals and groups associated with, or providing material support to, terrorist organizations and activities. This assistance is provided in the form of conducting intelligence/criminal financial investigations, financial analytical support, major case management, financial link analysis, and the deployment of teams of experts to develop investigative plans to analyze large volumes of documents and data. TFOS has provided this type of operational support in the Al Qa'ida sleeper cell cases in Buffalo and Portland, as well as in the Richard Reid, John Walker Lindh, Al Haramain, PIJ, and Mohamed Almoayad cases, among many others. This type of operational support has also been provided to Divisions investigating non-governmental organizations (NGOs), such as the Holy Land Foundation for Relief and Development, Benevolence International Foundation and the Global Relief Foundation.

•

6 The FBI conducted a detailed financial investigation/analysis of the19 hijackers and their support network, following the September 11th attacks. This investigation initially identified the Al Qa'ida funding sources of the 19 hijackers in the UAE and Germany. The financial investigation also provided the first links between Ramzi Binalshibh and the 9/11/01 terrorist attacks. A continuing investigation, in coordination with the PENTTBOMB Team, has traced the origin of the funding of September 11th back to financial accounts in Pakistan, where high-ranking and well-known Al Qa'ida operatives played a major role in moving the money forward, eventually into the hands of the hijackers located in the US. As part of the 9/11/01 financial investigation, thousands of individuals and organizations were investigated in the US and abroad to determine whether they played any part in supporting the hijackers or the operation. Although the vast majority of these individuals and

organizations were cleared, this process of elimination resulted in numerous other quality terrorism investigations being initiated, as well as criminal charges against hundreds of individuals for fraud and other criminal activity.

- 7 Since 9/11, the Treasury Department has frozen $36.3 million in terrorist assets, while the international community has frozen over $136 million, for a total of over $172 million.

- 8 The Treasury Department has issued blocking orders on the assets of more than 340 terrorists, terrorist organizations, and terrorist supporters, effectively denying them access to the US financial system.

- 9 Federal law enforcement officials have arrested over 61 individuals, indicted 43 and convicted 12 in connection with terrorist financing investigations.

- 10 US Government agencies, to include the FBI's TFOS, deployed trainers and advisers on missions to countries around the world to assist with the drafting of legislation to combat terrorist financing, strengthen bank supervision in identifying suspicious transactions, and address other financial crimes and corruption. Since 9/11/01, over 80 countries have introduced new terrorist-related legislation and approximately 84 countries established Financial Investigation Units.

- 11 As previously noted, TFOS has conducted near real-time financial tracking of a terrorist cell and provided specific and identifiable information to a foreign intelligence agency, which resulted in the prevention of six, potential deadly terrorist attacks.

- 12 In January 2003, the FBI, working in conjunction with German law enforcement, arrested Mohammed Al Hasan Al-Moayad, a Yemeni national, on charges of conspiring to provide material support to Al Qa'ida and Hamas. Al-Moayad was a significant financial contributor to Al Qa'ida and Hamas, and boasted he had provided over $20 million dollars to Usama Bin Laden. Al-Moayad participated in several fund-raising events at the Al Farouq Mosque in Brooklyn, NY. Al-Moayad was arrested during an undercover operation where he believed that he was to receive a large financial contribution, which he advised a source would be used to support mujahideen fighters of Al Qa'ida and Hamas. Along with Al-Moayad, several of his associates in New York were arrested for violating banking reporting requirements by structuring over $300,000 in several bank accounts in the United States.

- 13 In December 2002, a federal grand jury in Dallas returned an indictment against a senior leader of Hamas, Mousa Abu Marzouk, for conspiring to violate US laws that prohibit dealing in terrorist funds. Also charged and arrested by the FBI were Ghassan Elashi, the chairman of the Holy Land Foundation for Relief and Development, a charitable organization designated as a terrorist organization by the US Treasury Department's Office of Foreign Asset Control because of its fundraising activities on behalf of Hamas. Elashi and four of his brothers, all of whom are employees of the Richardson, Texas-based InfoCom Corporation, were charged with selling computers and computer parts to Libya and Syria, both designated state sponsors of terrorism. The indictment alleged that the Elashi brothers disguised capital investment from Marzouk, a specially designated terrorist for his admitted leadership role with Hamas, for their telecommunications company, InfoCom. The indictment and subsequent arrests have disrupted a US-based business, which was conducting its activities with a known Hamas leader and state sponsors of terrorism.

- 14 In October 2002, the FBI and other US government agencies assisted German authorities in identifying and taking legal action against Hamas in Germany. Through the efforts of the FBI, including TFOS, exchanges with Germany led to the closure of the Al-Aqsa Foundation in Germany, a suspected Hamas fundraising organization.

2. The use of information technology to better identify and isolate suspicious transactions related to terrorist financing

The FBI has a responsibility to be not only reactive but proactive as well, and to think strategically about potential threats and future case development. Accordingly, TFOS, together with the Counter-Terrorism Section, Criminal Division of the Department of Justice, has begun a number of proactive initiatives to identify potential terrorists and terrorist related financing activities.

The overriding goal of these projects is to proactively identify potential terrorists and terrorist related individuals, entities, mechanisms or schemes through the digital exploitation of data. To accomplish this, TFOS seeks to 1) identify potential electronic data sources within domestic and foreign government and private industry providers; 2) create pathways and protocols to legally acquire and analyze the data; and 3) provide both reactive and proactive operational, predictive and educational support to investigators and prosecutors.

Utilizing the latest computer technology available to the Counterterrorism Division, the Proactive Exploits Group (PEG) within TFOS serves as a proactive, financial intelligence investigative management and support team. PEG generates leads for TFOS and other FBI components. PEG also proposes and conducts proactive financial intelligence initiatives and projects. PEG works closely with TFOS operational units and document exploitation initiatives to ensure financial intelligence is being fully exploited and disseminated.

PEG has conducted an extensive review of data mining software and link analysis tools currently utilized by other governmental and private industries for consideration of use by the FBI. PEG also participates in the FBI's SCOPE Intelligence Data Warehouse (IDW) User Management Group and has been involved in the development and planning for future enhancements to the IDW. PEG has created an interactive, computer playbook generator that can assist investigators in determining data sources to be queried, based upon the quantity and quality of their investigative data.

PEG has initiated several projects to integrate data from TFOS' internal financial database, open/public source data and FBI and other government data sources onto a central query platform. Through this process, and in concert with contract vendors working for the SCOPE IDW Project, PEG has developed a process whereby the Financial Intelligence Analysis Unit (FIAU) within TFOS can batch query multiple databases for potential matches by names, telephone numbers, e-mails, etc. This batch process has the potential to save FIAU and the FBI hundreds, if not thousands, of hours of data input and query time on each occasion it is utilized. Furthermore, it facilitates rapid acquisition and sharing of information with other agencies. Through the sophisticated tools being utilized, and the matching protocols developed, FIAU can insure each query is properly conducted and done to a best practices query standard.

Recently, PEG utilized the batch process it developed to exploit over three thousand individual names, addresses, telephone numbers and e-mail addresses. The batch process accomplished in hours what would have taken TFOS personnel and FBI Field Offices over 4,300 man hours to conduct, potentially saving the FBI almost $70,000. Furthermore, because PEG conducted the queries in batch form, and has global access to all of the search results, previously unidentified links, patterns and associates among the data can now be extracted. Absent the batch process, this would have been extremely difficult, if not impossible, to accomplish.

PEG has initiated a variety of proactive data mining projects to identify potential terrorists and terrorist financing. The projects were conceived in 2002 and now, with the advent of certain software tools and data access, are either being implemented or will shortly begin. Some of the projects include the:

1 Social Security Number (SSN) Project

The SSN project is a multi-phase project that seeks to identify potential terrorist related individuals through SSN misusage analysis. SSNs identified as a result of terrorist related investigations are first provided to the Social Security Administration (SSA) for authentication. Once the validity or non-validity of the number has been established, investigators look for misuse of the SSNs by checking immigration records, Department of Motor Vehicle (DMV) records, and other military, government and fee-based data sources. Incidents of suspected SSN misusage are then separated according to type. Predicated investigative packages are then forwarded to the appropriate investigative and prosecutive entity for follow-up.

2 Suspicious Activity Report (SAR) Project

The SAR Project seeks to identify potential terrorists through the mining of the SAR database for key words, patterns, individuals, entities, accounts and specific numeric identifiers (i.e., Social Security; driver's license, passport, telephone and Immigration and Naturalization Service (INS) A numbers, etc.) The SAR Project looks for terrorist related activity among previously reported suspicious activity, regardless of whether it was identified with terrorism at the time of reporting. Incidents of suspected terrorist involvement are separated and, thereafter, forwarded to the appropriate investigative and prosecutive entity for follow-up. It is not always immediately apparent whether the reported SAR has a terrorism nexus. However, if the review is begun with predicated terrorism names and identifiers associated with terrorist investigations, the probability increases. PEG has assisted several individual FBI field offices in initiating their own versions of the SAR Project. Initial batch querying of the SAR database recently began, and analyses of the results are pending.

3 Terrorist Risk Assessment Model (TRAM)

•

TRAM seeks to identify potential terrorist and terrorism financing activity through the use of targeted, predictive pattern recognition algorithms. The project entails the compilation of past and current known data regarding individual and group terrorist activity, methodologies, demographics, financial patterns, etc., to form a predictive pattern recognition program. This risk assessment program could then be deployed against financial and other data to identify those pieces of information or persons that most closely resemble the pattern being sought after. The PEG will shortly begin a pilot testing of this capability to include the utilization of artificial intelligence and robotic searching models based on the patterns developed by TFOS.

•

•

4 Automatic/Robotic Playbook Generator

PEG has developed a computer database program that reviews Requests For Information (RFIs), determines what is requested and which FIAU contacts can provide potential answers to those questions. The computerized program then returns a "playbook", or set of instructions, the user can follow to gather the necessary information. Plans are underway to integrate this playbook generator with the batch process developed to automate much of TFOS' collection mechanisms. This will allow RFI's to be automatically processed, and the appropriate databases queried robotically.

It is important to understand that these projects and similar initiatives by TFOS seek only to more fully exploit information *already obtained* by the FBI in the course of its investigations or through the appropriate legal process, and where there is an articulated law enforcement need. TFOS does not seek access to personal or financial information outside these constraints.

3. 2003 National Money Laundering Strategy (with an emphasis on agency coordination)

With respect to the *2003 National Money Laundering Strategy*, I concur with the statements this morning of my colleagues as they relate to the strategy's goals and objectives. The blocking of terrorist assets worldwide, establishing and promoting of international standards for adoption by other countries to safeguard their financial infrastructures from abuse and facilitating international information are several key objectives which must be achieved if law enforcement and regulatory agencies are to have any success in stemming the flow of illegal funds throughout the world. Within the FBI, the investigation of illicit money flows crosses all investigative program lines. I would like to use my final moments with the Committees to share some examples of the Bureau's efforts towards coordination with other agencies so important to us in the fight against terrorism, recognizing that throughout my comments thus far this morning, our understanding and recognition of the need for the continued sharing of information, cooperation and outreach efforts are clearly noted.

Information sharing is critical to all of our efforts. The intelligence community, including the FBI, produces and obtains tremendous amounts of classified intelligence information. While much of the information can be of significant value in terrorist finance investigations, the value will not be realized or maximized absent the ability to filter the information, analyze it, and disseminate it in an appropriate manner to those who can make the best use of the information. Toward this end, TFOS participates in joint endeavors with the Treasury Department, the Department of Justice, and the Department of Homeland Security involving potential terrorist related financial transactions. TFOS also has personnel detailed to the CIA's Counter Terrorism Center, and personnel from there work directly with TFOS on financial intelligence matters.

In addition, the National Security Council formalized the Policy Coordinating Committee (PCC) on Terrorist Financing at the end of 2001. Treasury chairs the PCC, which generally meets at least once a month to coordinate the United States government's campaign against terrorist financing. The meeting generally focuses on ensuring that all relevant components of the federal government are acting in a coordinated and effective manner to combat terrorist financing.

The Departments of State, the Treasury, and Justice also established an interagency Terrorist Financing Working Group, chaired by the State Department, to coordinate government efforts to identify, prioritize and assess those countries that are vulnerable to terrorist exploitation. Groups of experts, including DOJ money laundering prosecutors, interagency law enforcement and regulatory members, have provided extensive on-the-ground assessments of such countries' vulnerabilities in an effort to develop and provide targeted training and technical assistance to those countries identified as most vulnerable.

Organizational changes have also taken place within the Executive Branch with respect to the investigation of terrorism financing, including the execution of a Memorandum of Agreement (MOA) between the Department of Justice (DOJ) and the Department of Homeland Security (DHS) concerning terrorist financing investigations. The MOA addressed the importance of waging a seamless, coordinated law enforcement campaign against terrorist sources of financing. Signed by Attorney General Ashcroft and Homeland Security Secretary Ridge on May 13, 2003, the FBI was designated to lead terrorist financing investigations and operations, while DHS would focus its law enforcement activities on protecting the integrity of US financial systems. To this end, DHS implemented "Operation Cornerstone", led by Immigration and Customs Enforcement (ICE), to identify vulnerabilities in financial systems through which criminals launder their illicit proceeds, bring them to justice and work to eliminate financial infrastructure vulnerabilities. Former US Customs Service "Operation Green Quest" criminal cases having no nexus to terrorism were converted to "Operation Cornerstone", while those cases having a nexus to terrorism were transitioned to the appropriate FBI Joint Terrorism Task Force (JTTF) having ICE participation. Ongoing and future "Operation Cornerstone" investigations that develop links to terrorism will be referred to the FBI through TFOS. ICE and TFOS are coordinating investigative initiatives that will enable ICE to identify financial systemic vulnerabilities, and which will enable TFOS to identify ties to terrorism and terrorist financing. In addition, there is a liaison from ICE assigned to TFOS, and investigators from ICE will be represented on the JTTFs.

Our efforts to combat terrorism have been greatly aided by the provisions of the PATRIOT Act and, pursuant to the *2003 National Money Laundering Strategy*, the FBI is ensuring its vigorous and appropriate application. The success in preventing another catastrophic attack on the US homeland would have been much more difficult, if not impossible, without the Act. It has already proved extraordinarily beneficial in the war on terrorism. Most importantly, the PATRIOT Act has produced greater collection and sharing of information within the law enforcement and intelligence communities.

Title III of the Act, also known as the International Money Laundering Anti-Terrorist Financing Act of 2001, has armed us with a number of new weapons in our efforts to identify and track the financial structures supporting terrorist groups. Past terrorist financing methods have included the use of informal systems for transferring value in a manner that is difficult to detect and trace. The effectiveness of such methods should be significantly eroded by the Act, which establishes stricter rules for correspondent bank accounts, requires securities brokers and dealers to file Suspicious Activity Reports or SARS, and money transmitting businesses, which include any person who engages as a business in the transmission of money, to register with FinCEN and file SARS.

There are other provisions of the Act that have considerably aided our efforts to address the terrorist threat including: strengthening the existing ban on providing material support to terrorists and terrorist organizations; the authority to seize terrorist assets; and the power to seize money subject to forfeiture in a foreign bank account by authorizing the seizure of a foreign bank's funds held in a US correspondent account.

The FBI has utilized the legislative tools provided in the USA PATRIOT Act to further its terrorist financing investigations. Some examples of how TFOS has used the provisions in the USA PATRIOT Act are: to obtain foreign bank account information by issuing administrative subpoenas on foreign banks' US correspondent banks; to corroborate financial data obtained through criminal investigative techniques with intelligence sources; and to provide grand jury material to a foreign intelligence agency. All of these techniques have significantly assisted ongoing terrorism investigations and would not have been possible, but for the enactment of the USA PATRIOT Act.

It is important for the Committee and the American people to know that the FBI is using the PATRIOT Act authorities in a responsible manner. We are making every effort to effectively balance our obligation to protect Americans from terrorism with our obligation to protect their civil liberties.

Terrorism represents a global problem. The solution is grounded in what would have been considered, prior to 9/11/01, unprecedented international cooperation and coordination. The threat it poses must always be considered imminent. In addition to considerable financial investigative expertise, addressing terrorism and the finances that support and propagate it requires the ability to both implement proactive and preventive approaches to disrupt and dismantle, as well as the ability to conduct highly reactive immediate response financial investigations to address potential imminent threats. As stated herein, and in conjunction with more and more of the international community and other aspects of the US Government, the FBI has made considerable progress toward achieving and implementing these abilities.

Again, I offer my gratitude and appreciation to you, Chairman Platts and Chairman Putnam, as well as the distinguished members of both Committees, for dedicating your time and effort to this issue, and I would be happy to respond to any questions you may have.

Mr. PUTNAM. Our next witness is Ms. Marcy Forman, Deputy Assistant Director for Financial Investigations Division, U.S. Immigration and Customs Enforcement at the Department of Homeland Security.

In this position, Ms. Forman has oversight on three specific initiatives under the Financial Investigations Division, the centerpiece of which is Cornerstone. Cornerstone focuses on identifying means and methods used by criminal organizations to exploit financial systems through the transfer, laundering, and/or concealment of the true source of criminal proceeds.

Welcome to the subcommittee. You are recognized.

STATEMENT OF MARCY M. FORMAN, DEPUTY ASSISTANT DIRECTOR, FINANCIAL INVESTIGATIONS DIVISION, U.S. IMMIGRATION AND CUSTOMS ENFORCEMENT, U.S. DEPARTMENT OF HOMELAND SECURITY

Ms. FORMAN. Thank you. Good morning, Chairman Putnam and Chairman Platts. It is a privilege to appear before you to discuss the ongoing law enforcement efforts and accomplishments of the Department of Homeland Security [DHS], Bureau of Immigration and Customs Enforcement [BICE]. BICE Financial Investigations is committed to protecting the integrity of America's financial systems against the exploitation by money launderers and those who finance terrorism.

I would like to begin by commending Congress for its decisive and immediate enactment of the USA Patriot Act, enabling law enforcement to more effectively investigate money laundering and terrorist finance activities in order to protect the financial systems of this Nation.

DHS fully supports the mission of BICE. Secretary Ridge demonstrated this commitment by participating in the rollout of BICE's Cornerstone initiative in July 2003, which I will discuss further in my testimony.

BICE is pleased to have the Department's full support in these investigations and in working cooperatively with the private sector to help reduce the vulnerabilities of the financial systems exploitation.

Financial investigations continue to be a BICE priority. BICE brings a unique assembly of over 30 years of financial investigative expertise, powerful statutory authorities and cutting-edge investigative techniques in the conduct of money laundering and terrorist financing investigations. The enactment of the USA Patriot Act serves to further enhance these investigative techniques.

The enactment of the Money Laundering and Financial Crimes Strategy Act in 1998, which mandated the National Money Laundering Strategy, serves as a blueprint for addressing investigative financial priorities.

BICE and the former U.S. Customs Service has time and again demonstrated its expertise in the kinds of complex, large-scale, and high-impact investigations that BICE continues today. For example, the BICE-led investigations in such cases as the BCCI in Tampa, Operation Greenback in South Florida, Operation Casablanca in Los Angeles, Operation Wirecutter in New York, Operation Green Mile in Phoenix, and the BICE-led initiatives in the

New York El Dorado Task Force. In these cases and initiatives alone, BICE, in conjunction with other Federal, State and local law enforcement, has seized approximately $900 million in criminal proceeds.

I would like to take a moment to highlight the ongoing successes of the El Dorado Task Force. The El Dorado Task Force was created in 1992 and is the largest and most prominent interagency money laundering task force in the country. One recent El Dorado investigation led to the guilty plea of Broadway National Bank for violations of the Bank Secrecy Act, and paid a $4 million fine, the most significant BSA-related prosecution in many years.

This task force has since been the model for the establishment of other money-laundering task forces throughout the law enforcement community. It also served as a template for the creation of the High Intensity Financial and Related Crimes Areas, HIFCAs, that were created as part of the National Money Laundering Strategy.

In response to the events of September 11, 2001, BICE, through the former Customs Service established Operation Green Quest. Operation Green Quest was an interagency task force designed to augment existing counterterrorism efforts by targeting financial networks through the application of a systems-based approach to following the money.

Operation Green Quest was committed to the identification, disruption, and dismantling of organizations which served as sources of terrorist funding. In connection with the consolidation within DHS, in May 2003 a memorandum of agreement was reached between DHS and DOJ to clarify the roles and responsibilities for terrorist financing investigations.

BICE adopted the successful methodology embodied in Operation Green Quest to the new financial initiative called Cornerstone, which was launched in July 2003. As part of this initiative, BICE has expanded the longstanding working partnership with the financial and trade sectors in an effort to identify and eliminate the vulnerabilities that can be exploited by criminal and terrorist organizations.

Through Cornerstone and its predecessors, BICE has achieved great success in identifying systems that have been used by narcotics traffickers, arms traffickers, and terrorist networks to finance terrorist activities. These systems include trade-based violations such as the black market peso exchange, the largest trade-based laundering system in the Western Hemisphere, the smuggling of bulk cash, misuse of money service businesses and the exploitation of charities and nongovernmental organizations. Since October 25, 2001, the combined efforts of Operation Green Quest and Cornerstone have resulted in the seizure of approximately $35 million, have led to the execution of 172 search warrants, 233 arrests, 163 indictments and 94 convictions.

With the integration of the statutory authorities and investigative tools from the former Customs Service and the former Immigration and Naturalization Service, BICE is able to more effectively target vulnerabilities that facilitate illegal activities.

Cornerstone systematically and strategically examines financial systems that may be susceptible to abuse and seeks to prevent their exploitation. In addition, Cornerstone relies on the worldwide network of 37 BICE foreign attache officers, which have established and continued to maintain criminal relationships for corresponding law enforcement government enemies in their host country.

I noted earlier a number of BICE investigative successes and would like to provide a brief outline of a few of our significant ongoing investigations. In northern Virginia, as a result of the BICE, IRS, and FBI ongoing investigations of charities and nongovernment organizations, Biheiri was convicted for various immigration violations. In addition, Alamoudi was arrested and indicted for violations of immigration law, money laundering, structuring transactions with the government of a state that supports terrorism, and the International Emergency Economic Powers Act [IEEPA].

It is alleged that these individuals and their organizations were financing terrorist groups around the world. In Miami, BICE detained and seized approximately $5.6 million in assets belonging to a high-ranking Nicaraguan Government official who was alleged to have embezzled and laundered in excess of $100 million. This investigation was conducted by the BICE-led Foreign Political Corruption Unit, in coordination with the BICE Attache Office/Panama, and the Nicaraguan Government.

In Seattle, 13 individuals were indicted for transferring $12 million to Iraq in violation of money laundering laws and IEEPA. To date, the primary subject of this suggestion has been convicted of money laundering and additional prosecutions are pending.

In the New York-Newark metropolitan area, BICE, together with IRS and other law enforcement agencies, conducted joint investigations which targeted money service businesses operating without a license. These investigations identified the illegal transfer of about $100 million to countries of interest.

To date, these investigations have resulted in 14 arrests, 12 indictments, 6 convictions for failure to register as a money service business, and for other violations.

With these investigations, BICE has demonstrated the benefits derived from the USA Patriot Act, specifically to the statutory changes related to unlicensed money service businesses, cash smuggling, and the expanded authority to identify accounts belonging to suspects. The BICE Financial Division has continuously evolved to match its investigative priorities with the critical concerns of this Nation.

Since March 2003, BICE Financial and Strategic Investigative Division has deployed four teams of BICE special agents to the Iraqi theater of operations. BICE special agents are conducting investigations relative to violations of U.S. law, to include weapons of mass destruction, illegal procurement of U.S.-origin technology, and money laundering.

BICE has established an Iraq task force in Washington, DC, to review and analyze documents and financial records that have been obtained through the world to identify violations of U.S. laws. To date, BICE special agents have been responsible for the recovery of over $32 million in cash hidden in Iraq by the former regime, and are attempting to determine the source of these funds.

As part of the DHS initiative to promote a partnership with the private financial sector, BICE, in coordination with the U.S. Secret

Service, will hold semiannual Systematic Homeland Approach to Reducing Exploitation [SHARE] meetings. SHARE meetings will promote an exchange of information between government and executive members of the financial and trade communities that are impacted by money laundering, identify theft, and various other financial crimes.

In support of SHARE, Cornerstone publishes Tripwire, a quarterly newsletter that BICE provides to the financial sector to address law enforcement concerns, emerging trends, patterns and pathologies in the money laundering and terrorist finance arena.

In conclusion, I would like to thank the chairmen for the opportunity to testify before you today. I would also like to thank the joint subcommittees for their continued interest and support. It would be my pleasure to answer any questions.

Mr. PUTNAM. Thank you, Ms. Forman.

[The prepared statement of Ms. Forman follows:]

TESTIMONY
OF
MARCY M. FORMAN
DEPUTY ASSISTANT DIRECTOR
FINANCIAL INVESTIGATIONS DIVISION
BUREAU OF IMMIGRATION AND CUSTOMS ENFORCEMENT
DEPARTMENT OF HOMELAND SECURITY

BEFORE THE
HOUSE COMMITTEE ON GOVERNMENT REFORM
SUBCOMMITTEE ON GOVERNMENT EFFICIENCY AND FINANCIAL MANAGEMENT
SUBCOMMITTEE ON TECHNOLOGY AND INFORMATION POLICY AND THE CENSUS

DECEMBER 15, 2003

I. Introduction

Good morning Chairman Putnam and Chairman Platts. It is a privilege to appear before you to discuss the ongoing law enforcement efforts and accomplishments of the Department of Homeland Security's (DHS) Bureau of Immigration and Customs Enforcement's (BICE) Financial Investigations Division. BICE Financial Investigations is committed to protecting the integrity of America's financial systems against the exploitation by money launders and those who finance terrorism. I would like to begin by commending Congress for its decisive and immediate enactment of the USA PATRIOT Act, enabling law enforcement to more effectively investigate money laundering and terrorist finance activities in order to protect the financial systems of this Nation.

DHS fully support this mission and BICE's efforts. Secretary Ridge demonstrated this commitment by participating in the rollout of BICE's Cornerstone initiative in July 2003, which I discuss later in my testimony. BICE is pleased to have the Department's full support in conducting these significant investigations and in working cooperatively with the private sector to help reduce the vulnerabilities of the financial system to exploitation.

Financial investigations continue to be a key BICE priority. BICE brings a unique assembly of over 30 years of financial investigative expertise, powerful statutory authorities, and cutting edge investigative techniques in the conduct of money laundering and terrorist finance investigations. The enactment of the USA PATRIOT Act serves to further enhance these investigative techniques available to law enforcement. The enactment of the Money Laundering and Financial Crimes Strategy Act in 1998, which mandated the annual Money Laundering Strategy served as a blue print for addressing investigative financial priorities.

BICE, and the former U.S. Customs Service, has time and again demonstrated its expertise in the kinds of complex large-scale and high-impact investigations that BICE continues to investigate today. For example, BICE led investigations in such cases as the Bank of Commerce and Credit International (BCCI) in Tampa; Operation Greenback in South Florida; Operation Casablanca in Los Angeles; Operation Wirecutter in New York; Operation Green Mile in Phoenix; and the BICE led New York El Dorado Task Force. In these cases and initiatives alone, BICE, in conjunction with other federal, state and local law enforcement, has seized approximately $900 million dollars in criminal proceeds.

I would like to take a moment to highlight the ongoing success of the El Dorado Task Force. The El Dorado Task Force was created in 1992 and is the largest and most prominent interagency money laundering task force in the country. One recent El Dorado investigation led to the guilty plea of Broadway National Bank for violations of the Bank Secrecy Act (BSA) and a $4 million fine, the most significant BSA-related prosecution in many years. This task force has since been the model for the establishment of other money laundering task forces throughout the law enforcement community. It also served as a template for the creation of the High Intensity Financial and Related Crimes Areas (HIFCA's) that were created as part of the National Money Laundering Strategy.

II. BICE Financial Investigations Division

In response to the events of September 11, 2001, BICE through the former Customs Service established Operation Green Quest. Operation Green Quest was an interagency task force designed to augment existing counter-terrorism efforts by targeting financial networks through the application of a "systems-based" approach to "follow the money." Operation Green Quest was committed to the identification, disruption and dismantling of organizations which served as sources of terrorist funding. In connection with the consolidation within DHS, in May 2003, a memorandum of agreement was reached between DHS and DOJ to clarify the roles and responsibilities for terrorist financing investigations.

BICE adopted the successful methodology embodied in Green Quest into the new financial initiative called "Cornerstone", which was launched in July 2003. As part of this initiative, BICE has expanded the longstanding working partnerships with the financial and trade sectors in an effort to identify and eliminate vulnerabilities that can be exploited by criminal and terrorist organizations.

Through Cornerstone, and its predecessors, BICE has achieved great success in identifying systems that have been misused by narcotics traffickers, arms traffickers and terrorist networks to finance their activities. These systems include trade-based violations, such as the Black Market Peso Exchange (BMPE), the largest known trade-based laundering system in the Western Hemisphere, the smuggling of bulk cash, the misuse of money service businesses, and the exploitation of charities and non-government organizations. Since October 25, 2001, the combined efforts of Green Quest and Cornerstone resulted in the seizure of approximately $35 million, and have led to 172 search warrants, 233 arrests, 163 indictments and 94 convictions.

With the integration of the statutory authorities and investigative tools from the former Customs Service and the former Immigration & Naturalization Service, BICE is able to more effectively target vulnerabilities that facilitate illegal activities. Cornerstone systematically and strategically examines financial systems that may be susceptible to abuse and seeks to prevent their exploitation. In addition, Cornerstone relies on the worldwide network of 37 BICE Foreign Attaché offices, which have established and continue to maintain critical relationships with corresponding law enforcement and government entities in the host country.

III. Investigative Successes

I noted earlier a number of ICE investigative successes and would like to provide a brief outline of a few of our significant ongoing investigations:

- In Northern Virginia as a result of the BICE, IRS, and FBI ongoing investigations of charities and non-government organizations, Soliman Biheiri was convicted for various Immigration violations. In addition, Abdurahman Alamoudi was arrested and indicted for violations of immigration law, money laundering, structuring, transactions with the government of a state that supports terrorism, and the International Emergency Economic Powers Act (IEEPA). It is alleged that these individuals and their organizations were financing terrorist groups around the world.
- In Miami, BICE detained and seized approximately $5.6 million dollars in assets belonging to a high-ranking Nicaraguan government official who is alleged to have embezzled and laundered in excess of $100 million. This investigation was conducted by the BICE led Foreign Political Corruption Unit, in coordination with the BICE Attaché Panama and the Nicaraguan government.
- In Seattle, 13 individuals were indicted for transferring $12 million to Iraq in violation of money laundering laws and IEEPA. To date, the primary subject of this investigation has been convicted of money laundering and additional prosecutions are pending.

- In the New York/Newark Metropolitan area, BICE, together with IRS and other law enforcement agencies, conducted joint investigations, which targeted money service businesses operating without a license. These investigations identified the illegal transfer of over $100 million to countries of interest. To date, these investigations resulted in 14 arrests, 12 indictments, and 6 convictions for failure to register as a money service business and for other violations.

Through these investigations BICE has demonstrated the benefits derived from the USA PATRIOT Act, specifically to the statutory changes related to unlicensed money service businesses, bulk cash smuggling, and the expanded authority to identify accounts belonging to suspects.

The BICE Financial Division has continuously evolved to match its investigative priorities with the critical concerns of this Nation. Since March 2003, BICE Financial and Strategic Investigative Divisions have deployed four teams of BICE Special Agents to the Iraqi Theater of Operations in support of Operation Iraqi Freedom. BICE Special Agents are conducting investigations relative to violations of U.S. law to include Weapons of Mass Destruction, illegal procurement of U.S. origin technology, and money laundering. BICE has established an Iraq Task Force in Washington, D.C. to review and analyze documents and financial records that have been obtained throughout the world to identify violations of U.S. laws. To date, BICE Special Agents have been responsible for the recovery of $32 Million in cash hidden in Iraq by the former regime and are attempting to determine the source of these funds.

As part of the DHS initiative to promote a partnership with private financial industries, BICE in coordination with the U.S. Secret Service will hold semi-annual Systematic Homeland Approach to Reducing Exploitation (SHARE) meetings. SHARE meetings will promote an exchange of information between government and executive members of the financial and trade communities that are impacted by money laundering, identity theft, and various other financial crimes. In support of SHARE, Cornerstone publishes "Tripwire," a quarterly newsletter that BICE provides to the financial sector to address law enforcement concerns, emerging, trends, patterns, and typologies in the money laundering and terrorist finance arena.

IV. Conclusion

In conclusion, I would like to thank the Chairmen for the opportunity to testify before you today and to highlight the investigative efforts and successes of the Bureau of Immigration and Customs Enforcement. I would also like to thank the joint Subcommittees for their continued interest and support. It would be my pleasure to answer any questions you may have.

Mr. PUTNAM. The financial witness is Mr. Bruce Townsend. Mr. Townsend is currently Deputy Assistant Director of the U.S. Secret Service Office of Investigations. A career member of the Senior Executive Service, he oversees Secret Service offices in the United States and in 20 countries abroad, he develops Secret Service investigative policy, and leads the investigative initiatives.

We welcome your input to the subcommittee and thank you for being here. You are recognized.

STATEMENT OF BRUCE TOWNSEND, DEPUTY ASSISTANT DIRECTOR, OFFICE OF INVESTIGATIONS, U.S. SECRET SERVICE, U.S. DEPARTMENT OF HOMELAND SECURITY

Mr. TOWNSEND. Good morning. Chairmen Platts and Putnam, thank you for the invitation to testify on the subject of terrorist financing and the role the Secret Service plays in combatting this problem.

With me today is Special Agent in Charge John Joyce of the Secret Service Tampa Field Office. I am pleased to report that our Tampa Field Office is fully engaged and committed to the interagency coordination that is necessary to assist in the effort to keep America secure.

In addition to providing the highest level of physical protection to our Nation's leaders, the Secret Service exercises broad investigative jurisdiction over a wide priority of financial crimes. As the original guardian of our Nation's financial payment systems, the Secret Service has a long history of pursuing those who would victimize our financial systems and the law-abiding citizens of the United States.

In recent years, the combination of the information revolution, the effects of globalization, and the rise of international terrorism have caused the investigative mission of the Secret Service to evolve dramatically. Today, our dual missions of investigations and protection have become fully interdependent and inseparable.

When the Secret Service moved from its home of 138 years in the Treasury Department to the Department of Homeland Security, we brought with us intact all of our personnel, resources, and investigative jurisdictions and responsibilities. Today those jurisdictions and responsibilities require us to be involved in the investigation of not only traditional financial crimes but also identity crimes, as well as a wide range of electronic and high-tech crimes.

The events of September 11, 2001 have altered the priorities and actions of law enforcement throughout the world, and the Secret Service is no exception. Immediately following the attacks, the Secret Service was able to bring its experience in credit card and identity fraud as well as its electronic crimes expertise to bear on the investigation, working with the Department of Justice, and the FBI in the following ways: Assisting in developing complete financial profiles of all suspects, living and deceased, in the investigation. Identifying other suspects through current and historical financial investigations. Contributing to an intelligence assessment regarding possible future acts through analysis of money movement, expenditures, and other financial data. Developing an analysis of current credit card usage by the suspects in the investigation.

Investigating more than 17,000 leads in support of the Department of Justice-led investigation.

As part of the Department of Homeland Security, the Secret Service continues to be involved in a collaborative effort targeted at analyzing the potential for financial, identity, and electronic crimes to be used in conjunction with terrorist activities.

The Secret Service prides itself on an investigative and preventative philosophy, which fully involves our partners in the private sector and academia and our colleagues at all levels of law enforcement in combatting the different types of financial and electronic crime committed against the people of the United States.

Central to our efforts in this arena are our liaison and information exchange relationships with the Treasury Department, the State Department, the FBI, and the Bureau of Immigrations and Customs Enforcement. As a key element in our strategy of sharing information and cooperating with other agencies involved in the effort to keep America safe, the Secret Service has assigned 58 special agents to the FBI's Joint Terrorism Task Forces, as well as headquarters personnel to the Bureau of Immigrations and Customs Enforcement [BICE], Operation Cornerstone, and the Treasury Department's Financial Crimes Enforcement Network [FinCEN].

It is through our work in the areas of financial and electronic crime that we have developed particular expertise in the investigation of credit card fraud, identify theft, cyber crime, and bank fraud. Secret Service investigative focus is often on organized criminal enterprises, both domestic and transnational.

As Secret Service investigations undercover activities of individuals or groups focusing on doing harm to the United States, appropriate contact is immediately made and information is passed to those agencies whose primary mission is counterterrorism. For more than a century, the Secret Service has maintained its dual missions of investigation and protection. Whether it is through the investigation of traditional financial and identity crime, the protection of our Nation's critical and financial infrastructure, or the safeguarding of our Nation's leaders, the Secret Service will continue to devote all its resources to assist in keeping the United States safe and secure from those wishing to do us harm.

Chairmen Platts and Putnam, this concludes my prepared statement. I will be pleased to answer any questions.

Mr. PUTNAM. Thank you very much, Mr. Townsend.

[The prepared statement of Mr. Townsend follows:]

Statement of Mr. Bruce A. Townsend

DRAFT

Deputy Assistant Director
Office of Investigations
United States Secret Service

Presentation to the Subcommittee on Government Efficiency and Financial Management and the Subcommittee on Technology and Information Policy and the Census

House Committee on Government Reform

U.S. House of Representatives

December 15, 2003

Chairman Platts, Chairman Putnam, Congressman Towns, Congressman Clay, and distinguished members of both subcommittees, thank you for inviting me to testify on the subject of terrorist financing and the role of the Secret Service in these investigations. With me today is Special Agent in Charge John Joyce of the Secret Service Tampa Field Office. I am pleased to report to the Committee that our Tampa Field Office is fully engaged and committed to the interagency coordination that is necessary to assist in the effort to keep America secure.

In addition to providing the highest level of physical protection to our nation's leaders, the Secret Service exercises broad investigative jurisdiction over a wide variety of financial crimes. As the original guardian of our Nation's financial payment systems, the Secret Service has a long history of protecting American consumers and industry from financial fraud. In recent years, the combination of the information revolution, the effects of globalization and the rise of international terrorism have caused the investigative mission of the Secret Service to evolve dramatically. Today, our dual missions of investigations and protection have become fully interdependent and inseparable.

After 138 years in the Treasury Department, the Secret Service transferred earlier this year to the Department of Homeland Security with all of our personnel, resources and investigative jurisdictions and responsibilities. Today, those jurisdictions and responsibilities require us to be involved in the investigation of traditional financial crimes as well as identity crimes and a wide range of electronic and high-tech crimes.

The events of September 11, 2001 have altered the priorities and actions of law enforcement throughout the world, and the Secret Service is no exception. Immediately following the attacks, the Secret Service was able to bring its experience in credit card and identity fraud as well as its electronic crimes expertise to bear on the investigation, working with the Department of Justice and the FBI, in the following ways:

- Assisting in developing complete financial profiles of all suspects (living and deceased) in the investigation;
- Identifying other suspects through current and historical financial investigations;
- Contributing to an intelligence assessment regarding possible future acts through analysis of money movement, expenditures and other financial data;
- Developing an analysis of current credit card usage by the suspects in the investigation; and
- Investigating more than 17,000 leads in support of the Department of Justice investigation.

Agency Coordination

As part of the Department of Homeland Security, the Secret Service continues to be involved in a collaborative effort targeted at analyzing the potential for financial, identity and electronic crimes to be used in conjunction with terrorist activities. The Secret Service prides itself on an investigative and preventive philosophy, which fully involves our partners in the private sector and academia and our colleagues at all levels of law enforcement in combating the myriad types of financial and electronic crimes. Central to our efforts in this arena are our liaison and information exchange relationships with the Department of the Treasury, the Department of State, the FBI and the Bureau of Immigration and Customs Enforcement (ICE).

As a key element in our strategy of sharing information and cooperating with other agencies involved in the effort to keep America safe, the Secret Service has assigned 58 Special Agents to the FBI's Joint Terrorism Task Forces (JTTFs) and additional personnel to Operation Cornerstone (led by the Bureau of Immigration and Customs Enforcement and the Treasury Department's Financial Crimes Enforcement Network (FinCEN)).

The Secret Service currently has 17 permanent foreign offices that support both our protective and investigative missions. Agents in these offices work in cooperation with host country law enforcement officials and contribute to international information sharing and training as well as criminal investigations. The Secret Service also provides training for counterfeit investigations, financial crimes and computer intrusions to our international law enforcement partners.

The Secret Service is actively involved with a number of government-sponsored initiatives. At the request of the Attorney General, the Secret Service joined an interagency identity theft subcommittee that was established by the Department of

Justice. This group, which is comprised of federal, state, and local law enforcement agencies, regulatory agencies, and professional organizations, meets regularly to discuss and coordinate investigative and prosecutorial strategies as well as consumer education programs.

In a joint effort with the Department of Justice, the U.S. Postal Inspection Service, the Federal Trade Commission and the International Association of Chiefs of Police, we are hosting Identity Crime Training Seminars for law enforcement officers. In the last two years we have held seminars for officers in Chicago, Dallas, San Francisco, Las Vegas, Des Moines, Washington D.C., Phoenix, New York, Seattle, San Antonio, and Providence. In the coming months we have training seminars scheduled in Orlando, Buffalo and Atlanta. These training seminars are focused on providing local and state law enforcement officers with tools and resources that they can immediately put into use in their investigations of identity crime. Additionally, officers are provided resources that they can pass on to members of their community who are victims of identity crime.

Operation Direct Action (ODA) is a task force comprised of the Secret Service and a number of private sector partners. The primary focus of this task force is to target organized criminal groups that are committing large scale financial fraud, specifically credit card "bust out" schemes, which may impact our nation's financial infrastructure. A credit card bust out scheme is a type of fraud where a criminal obtains multiple credit card accounts and manipulates the lines of credit that are established with each card. The criminal makes payments with convenience checks issued by another card or with Non-Sufficient Funds (NSF) checks drawn on one of his or her many bank accounts. The criminal is taking advantage of the lag time that will occur between when his accounts will be credited with the payment and when the issuing banks determine that the checks were bad.

The ODA task force is not focused on developing cases with terrorism or terrorist financing connections. However, information from any investigation developed through ODA with suspected terrorism connections will be shared with those agencies with primary counterterrorism responsibilities.

It is through our work in the areas of financial and electronic crime that we have developed particular expertise in the investigation of credit card fraud, identity theft, check fraud, cyber crime, false identification fraud, computer intrusions, bank fraud, and telecommunications fraud. Secret Service investigations typically focus on organized criminal groups, both domestic and transnational. As Secret Service investigations uncover activities of individuals or groups focusing on doing harm to the United States, appropriate contact is immediately made and information is passed to those agencies whose primary mission is counterterrorism.

It is clear that terrorists are likely using financial, identity and electronic crimes to finance, plan and execute attacks against Americans. In response, the Secret Service routinely receives requests for our agents with specialized skills and expertise in the areas of financial and electronic crimes to serve on multi-agency task forces. The experience of our personnel has proven to be valuable to counterterrorism task forces and investigations. By using the skills that we have developed in financial crime investigations, as well as leveraging the relationships we have formed with the financial services industry, we can contribute to efforts to combat terrorism and terrorist financing. These contributions manifest themselves in connections made between what appear to be traditional organized criminal groups and possible terrorist cells.

It has been our experience that the criminal groups involved in these types of crimes routinely operate in a multi-jurisdictional environment. This has created problems for local law enforcement agencies that generally act as the first responders to their criminal activities. By working closely with other federal, state, and local law enforcement, as well as international police agencies, we are able to provide a comprehensive network of intelligence sharing, resource sharing, and technical expertise that bridges jurisdictional boundaries. This partnership approach to law enforcement is exemplified by our financial and electronic crime task forces located throughout the country. These task forces primarily target suspects and organized criminal enterprises engaged in financial and electronic criminal activity that fall within the investigative jurisdiction of the Secret Service.

Members of these task forces, who include representatives from local and state law enforcement, prosecutors offices, private industry and academia, pool their resources and expertise in a collaborative effort to detect and prevent electronic crimes. The value of this crime fighting and crime prevention model has been recognized by Congress, which has authorized the Secret Service (pursuant to the USA/Patriot Act of 2001) to expand our electronic crime task forces to cities and regions across the country. Recently, four new Electronic Crimes Task Forces (ECTFs) were established in Dallas, Houston, Columbia (SC) and Cleveland, bringing the total number of such task forces to 13.

The Secret Service Electronic Crimes Task Force program bridges the gap between conventional cyber-crimes investigations and the larger picture of critical infrastructure protection. Secret Service efforts to combat cyber-based assaults that target information and communications systems supporting the financial sector are part of the larger and more comprehensive critical infrastructure protection and counterterrorism strategy.

We also recognize that our unique protective responsibilities, including our duties as the lead federal agency for coordinating security at National Special Security Events, demand heightened electronic security awareness and preparation. A well-placed cyber attack against a weak technology or support infrastructure could render an otherwise sound physical security plan vulnerable and inadequate.

It should be noted that deliberate infrastructure attacks, from whatever source, are likely to be first identified as a cyber or electronic crime incident and will probably be addressed by law enforcement personnel in the course of routine business.

Given this continuum and interplay between computer-based crimes and national security issues, the Secret Service recognizes its role in investigating and helping to prevent electronic attacks against our critical infrastructures.

When we arrest a criminal who has breached or disrupted a sensitive communications network and are able to restore the normal operation of the host, we believe we have made a significant contribution towards assuring the reliability of the critical systems our country relies upon on a daily basis. But greater satisfaction and success are achieved when a potentially devastating incident is prevented due to our prior involvement, participation or sharing of information.

Secret Service Operations

Following are examples that highlight our contributions to the efforts to combat terrorism and terrorist financing.

The value that the Secret Service is able to bring to these types of investigations is demonstrated in the recent success of the Joint Terrorism Task Force (JTTF) investigation into the group charged with providing material support for Al-Queda in the Buffalo, New York area. This investigation began in June of 2001 when an anonymous letter was sent to the FBI Buffalo Field Office, identifying a number of individuals who had traveled to Afghanistan to attend an Al-Queda training camp. The letter further identified additional subjects who had knowledge of the training or provided financial assistance to those traveling to Afghanistan.

The JTTF dispatched agents and officers throughout the region concentrating on eight individuals alleged to have traveled to the training camps. Task force members conducted surveillances, background investigations, and full financial examinations into the accounts of the 8 individuals believed to have traveled to the camps. The Secret Service, recognized by the task force as experts in financial investigations, was tasked with identifying the banking and credit card accounts for each of the suspects. Through the course of the investigation the Secret Service was able to identify over 150 bank accounts from which additional information such as cell phone numbers, email accounts, and credit card accounts were identified. This information led to additional addresses, communications and acquaintances of the subjects involved and was vital in bringing the case into focus.

On July 30 of this year, Secret Service Special Agent Kim M. Baglio of our Buffalo Field Office was recognized by Attorney General John Ashcroft for her contributions to this investigation and presented the Attorney General's Award for Exceptional Service.

To date, the first six defendants have plead guilty to Title 18, USC 2339 B and 2; Providing Material Support and Resources to a Foreign Terrorist Organization. Sentencing for the six defendants is scheduled to be completed by December of 2003.

This investigation is illustrative of the Secret Service's expertise in the areas of financial crimes and cyber-investigations which aid in the joint counterterrorism efforts of law enforcement in the United States.

In addition to the high tech crimes that pose a threat to the security of our nation's financial systems and critical infrastructure, the counterfeiting of U.S. dollars remains a - threat to our financial and national security. Counterfeiting of U.S. dollars by organized criminal groups poses a multi faceted threat to the United States and its allies.

The first and most obvious threat is to the integrity of U.S. banknotes themselves. Counterfeiting of U.S. dollars is a constant criminal concern, particularly with the expanded use of U.S. currency in those countries that have adopted the U.S. dollar as their own currency. Within these semi or fully-"dollarized" nations, large-scale counterfeiting operations such as those in Colombia have the potential to disrupt the economies of countries such as Ecuador, El Salvador and others in the Central and South American region.

At the present time, levels of counterfeiting do not have a major impact on the U.S. or world economy, although the loss represented by each counterfeit note is significant to the individual or business that receives it. However, confidence in the U.S. dollar draws countries, investors and individuals to use and hold dollars as a safe and secure currency. An influx of counterfeit U.S. dollars into an economy that is not fully dollarized, whether local or national, can adversely affect the individuals' confidence in U.S. currency. The influx of counterfeit may be real or perceived, as often times only a few counterfeit notes passed on a local economy creates the false perception of an epidemic. Nonetheless, confidence in the U.S. dollar is diminished and consumers begin using and holding other currencies.

On a national scale, this shift in confidence and the move to currencies that are perceived to be less vulnerable to counterfeiters and therefore more secure to the individual, results in fewer U.S. dollars circulating within that economy and ultimately a loss in segniorage revenues to the U.S. So, while the direct financial losses resulting from the passing and circulation of counterfeit currency remain low, the indirect losses may potentially be much greater.

The targeting of fully-dollarized economies by international counterfeiters presents additional concerns for the United States. An increase in the level of counterfeit U.S. dollars introduced into a fully-dollarized economy adversely affects the local confidence in the stability of U.S. currency. Again, whether the affects are real or perceived, the local perception is that U.S. dollars are no longer safe. As such, the reactionary price increase of goods and services in order to offset losses attributed to the circulation of counterfeit U.S. dollars can lead to inflation.

Since the 1989 appearance of a deceptive counterfeit U.S. banknote (sometimes referred to in the press as the "Supernote") the Secret Service has been investigating the involvement of North Korea in the manufacturing and distribution of counterfeit U.S. currency.

In the last 14 years, fourteen additional variations (referred to as circulars) have been identified and linked together either through forensic or investigative associations. The manufacturers of this family of counterfeit notes utilize complex and expensive printing techniques such as intaglio and typographic. The sophisticated printing method is evidence of a well-funded, ongoing, organized criminal enterprise, with a significant scientific and technological component.

Mr. Chairman, the information regarding this family of counterfeit notes is being presented as an extremely brief overview of North Korea's involvement in the manufacturing and distribution of counterfeit U.S. Federal Reserve Notes. The Secret Service would welcome the opportunity to provide the committee with additional information regarding this investigation in another forum.

Recent investigations have shown a significant level of counterfeiting-related activity in the tri-border area of Brazil, Argentina and Paraguay. As an area with an extensive history of narcotics trafficking and other border crime and a reputation for lawlessness, the tri-border area is of continued interest to the law enforcement and intelligence communities.

The pre-war Iraqi dinar, which is essentially valueless, is known to be used by Colombian counterfeiters as a currency paper to print counterfeit U.S. currency (after the ink is chemically removed from the Iraqi dinar paper). Although no formal connection has been established, this potential link between other groups operating in the tri-border region and the Colombian counterfeiting groups presents a concern for law enforcement and intelligence officials in the United States and South America.

We will aggressively investigate any relationship between Colombian criminal groups and groups operating in the tri-border region. While traditionally these activities have been limited to Colombia and the Central and South American regions; recent statistics have shown statistical increases in counterfeit activity in other locations throughout the world such as Pakistan, Afghanistan, and even Chechnya. Again, although there is no established connection between transnational counterfeiting and terrorism, we will continue to be vigilant in our investigations and recognize that the potential exists for terrorists to use new methods to finance their operations.

An example of the Secret Service's success in this region can be seen in the results of "Plan Colombia". Through the State Department's Plan Colombia, the Secret Service's goal was to further train and equip a vetted anti-counterfeiting force to work in conjunction with the Secret Service in the seizure and suppression of counterfeit U.S. dollars manufactured in Colombia. For almost thirty years, Colombia has remained the largest producer of counterfeit U.S. currency in world. Through the funding provided under "Plan Colombia," the Secret Service and Colombian law enforcement authorities were able to make a tremendous impact on the counterfeiters, their distribution networks, and ultimately, the amount of Colombian manufactured counterfeit U.S. dollars that reached the streets of the United States.

Since the program's inception, our joint efforts have led to the seizure of $123.3 million in counterfeit U.S. currency, the suppression of 33 counterfeit printing plants, and over 164 arrests.

As stated before, the Secret Service is also involved in investigations of transnational organized criminal groups who use financial, electronic and identity crimes not only for monetary gain but also to commit other types of crime. An ongoing case illustrates the transnational nature of certain Middle Eastern organized criminal enterprises and the alliances formed between groups in order to further their activities. These different organized groups, allied together, present a non-traditional organized crime structure that can be viewed as cellular in nature. Although I cannot discuss the details of this ongoing case, the investigation is targeting over 80 subjects in states all across the U.S. for crimes such as counterfeit checks, false identification fraud, cigarette bust out schemes, access device fraud and skimming, mail theft, bank fraud, arson and narcotics trafficking. In this case, most of the illegal proceeds from these crimes are being sent overseas using various methods. Thus far in this multi-agency investigation we have determined that these groups are responsible for millions of dollars in losses.

Another example of organized criminal groups exploiting technology for criminal gain is the ATM fraud case that is ongoing in New York, Florida, and California. An organized criminal group from Eastern Europe purchased over 50 ATM machines and placed them in various locations around these states. As unsuspecting victims used their ATM cards in what they believed were legitimate ATM's, the electronic data contained on the back of their card, as well as their PIN numbers, were stolen. Over the course of several months over 21,000 individuals accounts were compromised from over 1,400 different banks. This organized criminal gang would then make counterfeit ATM cards encoded with the stolen information and withdraw money from the victim's accounts. Over $8.0 million has been lost to this group to date. Various members of this group have been arrested by our agents and, just recently, another prime suspect was arrested in the Midwest. We are working with the financial services industry and the Electronic Funds Transfer Association to assist in creating and tightening regulations to help prevent this kind of abuse of the system in the future.

Technology

The Secret Service has approximately 3,200 Special Agents. We have extensive experience and expertise in the areas of financial, identity and electronic crime investigations. Forming innovative task forces between the public and private sector, such as our network of Electronic Crimes Task Forces across the country, is one way we can contribute to the goal of keeping the American homeland safe and secure. Another is to share information with and develop tools and resources for law enforcement officers all across the country. In essence, this is acting as a "force multiplier" by sharing the knowledge, experience and expertise we have developed over the years of conducting financial and electronic crime investigations.

We have also attempted to provide information and resources to our law enforcement partners at the local and state level and to make that information instantly accessible. The E-information Network is a Secret Service Internet site specifically designed for law enforcement officers and financial institution investigators. Access to the site is free once officers and investigators are approved by the Secret Service. Information and alerts concerning all types of financial, identity and electronic crimes is located on the E-Information Network. Features of the E-Information Network include a counterfeit check database, a credit card site with Bank Identification Number search capability, a fictitious instruments section, a counterfeit and genuine documents database, and a reference library. Every law enforcement officer in the country can have their own user name and password for the Secret Service E-Information Network. Sharing information, tools and resources with all levels of law enforcement is vital and the Secret Service takes that responsibility very seriously.

In March of 1999, the Secret Service introduced a new web-based database offering a means for domestic and foreign law enforcement as well as the financial community to conduct searches of suspected counterfeit notes against the Secret Service counterfeit note databases online. This website provides users with the ability to receive real-time verification of counterfeit notes that are of record with the Secret Service. Additionally, users can find information regarding the genuine security features of United States currency. There are now over 11,000 authorized users of this website worldwide.

Criminals increasingly employ technology as a means of communication, a tool for theft and extortion, and a repository for incriminating information. As a result, our investigations routinely involve the seizure and analysis of electronic evidence. In fact, so critical was the need for basic training in this regard that the Secret Service joined forces with the International Association of Chiefs of Police and the National Institute for Justice to create the "Best Practices Guide to Searching and Seizing Electronic Evidence" which is a guide designed for the first responder, line officer and detective alike. This guide assists law enforcement officers in recognizing, protecting, seizing and searching electronic devices in accordance with applicable statutes and policies.

We have also worked with these same partners in producing the interactive, computer-based training program known as "*Forward Edge*," which takes the next step in training officers to conduct electronic crime investigations. *Forward Edge* is a CD-ROM that incorporates virtual reality features as it presents three different investigative scenarios to the trainee. It also provides investigative options and technical support to develop the case. Copies of state computer crime laws for each of the fifty states as well as corresponding sample affidavits are also part of the training program and are immediately accessible for instant implementation. Over eight hours of training is available from the Forward Edge CD-ROM.

Thus far, we have distributed, free of charge, over 300,000 "Best Practices Guides" to local and federal law enforcement officers and as well as over 30,000 *Forward Edge* training CDs.

Additionally, this past year we have developed the Identity Crime Interactive Resource Guide CD-ROM which contains over 50 investigative and victim assistance resources that local and state law enforcement officers can use when combating identity crime. This CD-ROM also contains a short identity crime video that can be shown to police officers at their roll call meetings which shares what other departments are doing to combat identity crime and what tools and resources are available to officers. The Identity Crime CD-ROM is an interactive resource guide that was made in collaboration with the U.S. Postal Inspection Service, the Federal Trade Commission and the International Association of Chiefs of Police.

We have sent an Identity Crime Interactive Resource Guide CD-ROM to every law enforcement agency in the United States. Departments can make as many copies of the CD-ROM as they wish and distribute this resource to their officers to use in identity crime investigations. Over 70,000 Identity Crime CD-ROMs have been produced and distributed.

As you know, Mr. Chairman, Congress is currently considering legislation that establishes increased penalties for aggravated identity theft -- that is, identity theft committed during and in relation to certain specified felonies. This proposal provides for two years imprisonment for the identity crime in addition to the punishment associated with the related felony, and five years imprisonment if the related felony is associated with terrorism. Additionally, the legislation prohibits the imposition of probation and allows for consecutive sentences. While this particular legislation cannot be expected to completely suppress identity theft, it does recognize the impact identity theft has on consumers and the need to punish those engaging in criminal activity for personal or financial gain. The Secret Service supports these ideas and believes they represent additional tools that law enforcement can utilize to the fullest extent in protecting the American people.

For more than a century the Secret Service has maintained its dual missions of investigation and protection. Whether it is through the investigation of traditional financial and identity crime, the protection of our nation's critical and financial infrastructure or the safeguarding of our nation's leaders, the Secret Service will continue to devote all its resources to assist in keeping the United States safe and secure from those wishing to do us harm.

Chairman Platts and Chairman Putnam, this concludes my prepared statement. Thank you again for this opportunity to testify on behalf of the Secret Service. I will be pleased to answer any questions at this time.

Mr. PUTNAM. And thank you to all of our witnesses. And this lays the foundation for I think an important dialog. And we will let Mr. Platts begin with the questions. You are recognized.

Mr. PLATTS. Thank you, Mr. Chairman. And, again, my thanks to each of you for your testimonies and participation.

Maybe start with kind of a broader question regarding the National Money Laundering Strategy. And all are free to answer. But I think, Mr. Ross, and Ms. Forman, Mr. Whitehead, it kind of directly relates to your three entities.

Currently, just the Department of Justice and Treasury sign off on that strategy. With the realignment of duties and with BICE being at DHS and Secret Service being at DHS, it seems logical if we are going to reauthorize the strategy, now that this initial 5-year period is up, that we would look at having DHS be one of the signatories to that strategy, given the important role that DHS plays in this issue.

I would be interested in the perspective of each of your offices in adding DHS as one of the three signatories, instead of just two.

Mr. ROSS. Thank you, Mr. Chairman. I agree with you. I think, if it is reauthorized—and I understand Senator Grassley has a bill that would reauthorize the Money Laundering Strategy, I think through 2006. I agree with you.

I think, given the competences and the capabilities that have been transferred from Treasury over to DHS, particularly the antimoney-laundering areas described by Ms. Forman on Cornerstone, I think DHS is an integral player to the money laundering strategies.

In fact, they were consulted with respect to this one. I think the timing was just such that the signature wasn't there. But I concur. The Treasury Department concurs.

Mr. PLATTS. Mr. Whitehead, for Justice. Any objections to DHS having to sign off as well?

Mr. WHITEHEAD. Well, clearly DHS is an important part of the equation. And I think, as Mr. Ross said, it was probably a timing issue there as for when the first agreement was signed. So there would be no objections, from my perspective. Of course I am looking at it from the local perspective, but, nationally, I wouldn't see where there would be an opposition to that.

Mr. PLATTS. I assume, Ms. Forman, DHS would like to have a greater say in that strategy if it is to be reauthorized. And maybe if you want to speak also to the issue—and, if others want to add as well—should we be reauthorizing it in a similar form to what it is, or should we look at some significant changes, given the events of the last 5 years?

Ms. FORMAN. To answer the first question, I agree DHS should be an integral part of the Money Laundering Strategy, and I believe we will be, based on the historical perspective as well as our current perspective in money laundering investigations.

With regards to the reissuance of a National Money Laundering Strategy, I certainly would support it with some modifications in terms of probably greater accountability in terms of the participants, agents, as well as a proposal for some funding resources to go along with it.

Mr. PLATTS. And accountability for developing better performance standards, kind of how to judge what everyone is bringing to the table? In what sense would you envision more accountability?

Ms. FORMAN. Performance standards as well as compliance with the dictates and the agreements in the strategy, and based on the goals and objectives that are set forth, to make sure that we are in concert in reaching those goals and objectives.

Mr. PLATTS. That kind of begs the question: Are there specific examples that you believe now we are not doing that, that we are not—all entities that are part of the strategy are not complying with all of the aspects of the strategy?

Ms. FORMAN. No. I think all of the agencies are in—going in the direction to achieve those. But I think we need to prioritize in terms of which ones we can achieve realistically during the timeframes that are set out.

Mr. PLATTS. Any other comments on maybe the reauthorization? Any changes from what we currently have, if we are going to reauthorize?

Mr. ROSS. One point I would like to make since the fact that since September 11, it has been a greater emphasis, obviously, on terrorist financing. As everyone has testified, the systems that are utilized by terrorist financiers and the systems that are utilized by money launders are virtually the same. There are different players involved. For instance, you don't usually find narcotraffickers using charities to move narcoproceeds.

But the systems themselves, the bulk couriers, the money remitters, the money order sales, the international movements of funds, the systems are the same. So I think that to the extent that it is reauthorized, it would not be untoward to maintain a terrorist financing component within the strategy itself, as we have done.

With respect to changes, I think a yearly report in a lot of cases causes some of the tensions that Ms. Forman was talking about, and that possibly something along the line of a different yearly report, a yearly report in a little different timeframe than February, might be something to consider with respect to the strategy. And also additional resources and funding, I think are important, particularly, if we are—if Congress is looking to reauthorize a continuation of the HIFCA-type program.

As you know, setting up a program with no funding and no resources and kind of on a voluntary basis is very difficult at best, and in some circumstances could suggest, you know, taking from Peter to pay Paul, and that sort of thing. So I think funding and resources would be an area in which we would like to work closely with Congress if it is determined to reauthorize.

Mr. PLATTS. And, Mr. Ross, you kind of touched on a followup I had, was with the funding issue, with the HIFCAs. And if we are reauthorizing and continue that mandate, should, one, there be a dedicated funding stream for that requirement, and should HIFCAs be part of that reauthorization, given how they have been used thus far?

Mr. ROSS. I think in the HIFCA context, a lot of it has been determined by what existed before, as opposed to what you are trying to recreate. As Ms. Forman testified, the El Dorado Task Force was kind of the paradigm example of an interagency financial task force that preexisted. It became kind of the centerpiece with respect to the HIFCA.

The program, it was a fairly easy transition. In other areas where you did not have a specific interagency approach to financial crime, it is more difficult to try to pull the pieces together. And I think there, if you have a greater system accountability, as Ms. Forman said, and also funding, I think it will greater enable the districts and geographic areas of a sense of how they want to function, how do they want to pull together, what do they want to concentrate on? Do they want to specialize in narcotics money laundering? Do they want to specialize across the board?

I think that we do need to add some form and structure. Treasury will work—delighted to work very closely with all committees of the Congress as this goes forward.

Mr. PLATTS. I have one more kind of broad issue, and then yield back to the chairman. We are going to have several rounds. I appreciate your allowing us that, and your patience, as we do have a lot of questions.

When we look at—and we have had I believe tremendous success, knowing that we have a deadly enemy out there that, if given the opportunity to have another September 11th, would have it tomorrow if they could pull it off. And we need to be grateful for the work of our Intelligence Community, our law enforcement community, our military, that have taken the fight to Osama bin Laden and al-Qaeda instead of waiting for them to bring the fight to us again.

But, as we are always looking to improve in how to strengthen our abilities, and while we are grateful for the successes over the last plus 2 years, one of the things that when I look at the reorganization, when we created the Department of Homeland Security, was to really try to bring together under that one roof the various entities involved in this battle and this war on terror. And with, you know, the historic move of Secret Service from Treasury to DHS, Immigration and Customs, the various aspects that were consolidated—and then we have the memorandum of agreement this summer that kind of undoes what I thought that we were doing with the creation of the Department and the shift of the criminal investigation responsibility out of the Department to the FBI and the Department of Justice, which seems to negate the advantages of DHS, especially with Treasury and BICE being in DHS.

I welcome all of your comments on have we consolidated and then, in the end, decentralized through that memorandum of agreement. And maybe it ties into State as well, by the fact that we now have the FBI with the lead on criminal investigations, we have DHS and BICE kind of on the—guarding the framework, protecting the framework of the financial community, and then we have State chairing the Terrorist Financing Working Group that kind of brought everyone together, then through that kind of agreement have gone the opposite way.

Am I missing something in that belief?

Mr. TOWNSEND. Mr. Chairman, I will kick that one off. With regard to the Secret Service specifically, when the agreement that you are referring to was first contemplated, there was some initial confusion, and part of that is it was on the part of our own organization.

But that MOA—and again speaking from the Secret Service perspective—has not affected us. We are carrying on with the historic and traditional missions that I mentioned in my opening statement.

I had an opportunity to speak to Mr. Ross prior to beginning today, from the Treasury Department. We have a special agent that continues to work in the Treasury Department on issues, and he brings information back and forth as is needed. And we intend to enhance that relationship both in staffing and the quality of the relationship.

So we are while, we hope, contributing to the new mission of the Department, we believe that we can make a contribution there, we are certainly endeavoring to do whatever we can to bring whatever expertise and resources we have to the Department and thereby keeping America safe, we still are continuing with our historic mission.

One, probably the most illustrative, is that of the integrity of our U.S. Federal Reserve notes, our bank notes. The Secret Service continues to work very closely with Treasury in tracking counterfeiting, both domestically and around the world. We are happy to report that while it is always a concern, the U.S. bank note and the U.S. currency is safe, sound, and secure. People want the dollar around the world. And they use it, and they should continue to do so.

So from the Secret Service perspective, clearly September 11 has changed everything, but at the same time, we continue to do the things we do best, but with a new focus on keeping the country safe.

Mr. PLATTS. OK.

Ms. FORMAN. If I may address that question, the May 2003 memorandum of understanding created an environment of efficient and timely exchange of information. The document itself has a subset of protocols which establish the mechanisms of which information is exchanged and who will work what investigation based on various factors, to include what is in the best interests of the U.S. Government, the equities of the investigative agency, the resources expended, and the corporate knowledge.

And there are protocols in place where we have a deputy at TFOS is a BICE senior manager from the Financial Investigations Division. So we have unfettered access to information, and so does the FBI in the exchange of information regarding terrorist financing investigations.

We are still in the game of investigating terrorist financing as well as other vulnerabilities in a coordinated effort with the FBI. In addition, our methodology is the same. For the last 30 years, the former Customs Service, now BICE, has applied a methodology of attacking systems and identifying vulnerabilities in systems to include a corrupt system such as the black market peso exchange, to legitimate financial systems, such as the money service businesses, where in Phoenix, AZ we have a major initiative called BICE Storm, where we have identified money orders that are being utilized for alien smuggling as well as narcotics traffickers, based on an assessment of the system as well as a census that was conducted. So the methodology has always been the same.

We will go after the corrupt system if the entire system is corrupt, or we will surgically go in and remove the bad apple, that individual and entities that are corrupt.

Mr. WHITEHEAD. First off, the memorandum of agreement has clearly improved the coordination and development of the TFOS. And, as Ms. Forman stated, the exchange of personnel from BICE has really served to help to move that forward. I have a member of our TFOS, the unit chief, Frank Fabian, here. I would like to yield to him to make a couple of comments about that.

Mr. PUTNAM. We need to swear you in.

[Witness sworn.]

Mr. PUTNAM. Note for the record that he responded in the affirmative. If you will speak into the mic, please.

Mr. FABIAN. Certainly. In listening to the comments of Ms. Forman, I certainly echo those comments. And I would add that since the adoption of the MOA, we have put in place senior people over with BICE, as they have with us. We have established a joint vetting unit to ensure that cases that come in from the field are reviewed at the senior level in Washington.

Those cases that on the surface do not appear to have a terrorism financing nexus to them, are certainly then investigated through Homeland Security and BICE. Those that do, they continue to participate on through the JTTFs and respective field offices where they occur.

What this has done, in our opinion, is what it was set out to accomplish. And that is, to make sure that efforts were not duplicated by different agencies working the same cases perhaps from a different perspective, and maybe even not knowing that they were investigating them. So I think it has done a great deal to aid in the efficiency of the investigative efforts between the very talented agents that have for years been working these sorts of investigations through operation Green Quest, and now Cornerstone, with agents from the Bureau and the other participating agencies on the JTTF.

Mr. PLATTS. Well, I appreciate your addressing that. I think that is an important message to get out, that we have done our best to kind of break down those stovepipes and have all entities working hand in hand, and have the—in the end, all of us on the same page as we look out for the best interests of our fellow citizens.

Now I will reserve the rest of my questions for the next round. Thank you, Mr. Chairman.

Mr. PUTNAM. Thank you. The purpose of this hearing is to discuss the various schemes that terrorists and others have used to circumvent the existing regulatory framework to fund their illegal activities. And Mr. Ross, I think, has pointed out the similarities and the differences between traditional money laundering of moneys, profits generated by illegal activities, and terrorist financing, which also has that component but also may utilize profits that were very legitimately earned and funneled through charitable organizations or front groups.

The GAO report that was just released this weekend discussed another key component of the circumvention, and that involves methods other than using U.S. currency. The conversion of that currency into cigarettes, diamonds, gold, other species, if you will, that is easy to conceal, easy to transfer across borders. And it identified that as a weakness, that we may not have the current regulatory framework in place, which I would view as being an indication of success that our currency laws, whether it is bank secrecy or Graham-Leach-Bliley, or the Patriot, or the whole laundry list of things that have developed since the early 1970's, have pushed the bad guys into an alternative form of financing.

But I would ask—I suppose we will begin with Treasury and Customs or whomever is appropriate to address this issue of how effectively does the law allow us to track the transfer of commodities, which has become the alternative to using currency in some cases?

Mr. ROSS. Thank you, Mr. Chairman. I echo your views that to the extent that we have driven terrorist financiers and narcotraffickers and other organized criminals out of the direct banking and formal financial system, and even to a lesser extent out of the informal system and into a trade-based system, it is an accomplishment.

At the same time, it is not an end in and of itself. As Ms. Forman testified earlier, we at Treasury and now DHS and Justice are well aware of the use of trading commodities. We are well aware that, for instance, narcotraffickers move billions of dollars' worth of U.S. dollars back into Colombia in the form of trade goods. We are aware of that. We are working on it in an interagency basis.

I will defer to Ms. Forman to describe a particular mechanism that they have in place at DHS, I think it is the paradigm data base, to try to identify trade-based anomalies. But I will go specifically to the diamonds and commodities mentioned in the GAO report.

I think it is unfortunate that at the time the GAO report was finalized, the Money Laundering Strategy had not been released or not been released sufficient so that GAO could take a look at the report. In the strategy in appendix D we do have the report on trade-based money laundering and terrorist financing.

What we identify in that is that, of course, the use of commodities is to be expected. A, they are mediums of exchange in areas which are particularly susceptible to terrorist financing; that is, the Middle East, Africa, and the Far East. So the mechanisms are in place. The dealers are in place, people who have historically dealt in trade goods, diamonds, emeralds, gold, in particular are in place. And we do discuss this in the Money Laundering Strategy.

I think from a law and regulatory perspective that we do have the tools. I believe what we need to do more of is work more closely with our international counterparts because, as a member of the panel earlier mentioned, I guess Mr. Glass, as much money as is generated in the United States goes into terrorist financing, much, much more is generated abroad. What we need is for our international partners to identify and target the possible use of trade-based money laundering and terrorist financing through their countries as well.

But appendix D does address this topic.

Mr. PUTNAM. Ms. Forman.

Ms. FORMAN. If I could add. I concur with Mr. Ross's assessment in terms of having the tools necessary to identify trade-based money laundering. Customs, former Customs Service, now BICE, has a system called the numerically integrated intelligence system. It is a software package that was developed by former Customs Service, which is able to identify anomalies in trade. The software, it is a software package that contains Bank Secrecy Act data, import-export data, I–94 Immigration data, and various other type of data that can be utilized to identify anomalies in trade.

The benefit of having this software is when you are working with your international counterparts—and specifically I can site examples of us working with Colombia—in which we also have their trade data. So we are able to identify exports out of the United States, and the foreign country is able to identify what they actually received. Colombia, in particular, is indicative that when a certain amount of exports leave the United States, some commodities such as appliances, computers, and so forth may be smuggled in to avoid taxes and duties in Colombia, when, in fact, may be part of the black market peso exchange, or drug dollars, unwittingly used most of the time, are utilized to purchase these commodities.

Mr. PUTNAM. Anyone else? Mr. Glass.

Mr. GLASS. We at the State Department, we have been in touch with a number of organizations and governments around the world on the issue of alternative remittance systems and their reported use. There have been a variety of press reports about this over the past year or so. And it is an issue that we have, with other agencies, tried to gather and collect more information on.

It is an issue that is very, very difficult to get what I would call actionable intelligence on. It is an issue that—where there are a lot of stories, there is a lot of unsubstantiated information out there. And we are working and trying to get that more precise.

When we take action overseas in the realm of terrorist finance of any kind, whether it be against an entity or an individual or whatever, one of the things that is most important in that effort is providing information, a justification as to what you are doing and why you are doing it.

We often provide to overseas governments a statement of case as to why you suspect this activity is taking place by this organization or by this individual. And the point of this is we need hard information, not only of an intelligence nature, but information that is sharable with other governments, with organizations, to get them to act. It is one of the things that we are constantly pressing for in our interagency collaboration. We work with all of the agencies at this table on a routine basis in order to develop just that kind of information. But particularly when we get into the realm of alternative remittance systems, it becomes more and more of a challenge.

We do have in place, which I am sure that you are aware of, the Kimberly process to deal with conflict diamonds, where there is a certification regime on rough diamonds, in order to try to make it more difficult to use diamonds and gems to avoid the formal financial systems.

There is perhaps, however, more that can be done in the alternative remittance systems field. It is something where we do have ongoing discussions not only with our posts overseas, but also with a number of other governments around the world in order to come to terms with this important issue.

Mr. PUTNAM. Well, GAO devotes a considerable amount of space to this issue. It is clear that it is a main avenue of diversion. And its center of activity is in parts of the world where we, frankly, don't have a very large or active role: West Africa, essentially no government, no borders, no control, and a fair amount of the world's diamonds. And all indications are that they are funding al-Qaeda, Hamas, Hezbollah, among others. So it appears to be a gaping hole in our preparedness.

Speaking of international cooperation, how has international cooperation changed since September 11th, and the Patriot legislation? Who is cooperating the best? And who is cooperating the least?

Mr. GLASS. I presume that would be to the State Department?

Mr. PUTNAM. Give us your best diplomatic answer on who is.

Mr. GLASS. Well, I will tell you quite frankly, to my knowledge, before the Executive order of September 23, 2001, I am not aware that the State Department went out worldwide to every government in the world and asked them to freeze assets of a given entity or individual. This was something that really was a new undertaking in the aftermath of September 11th.

When the President signed the Executive order and included the 27 names in the annex to that Executive order, we immediately approached every country in the world and asked them to search these names, and said, if you find any assets from these individuals, they should be frozen.

And since that time, as I mentioned in my testimony, we have gone out over 75 times to every country with whom we have diplomatic relations around the world and asked them to freeze assets. We have provided them supporting information, we have provided them identifying information on each of those names and asked them to take action.

So we really do have, in many ways, much more of an international effort, if you will, a very precise and targeted effort against specific targets to freeze assets than was there at any time previously. This has worked I think in a promising way. Some two-thirds of assets frozen around the world have been frozen outside of the United States, one-third inside the United States, roughly speaking.

Assets are frozen at the current time in approximately 50 countries around the world, and about 170 countries report that they are taking action to freeze assets every time the names are released. Now, when names are added to the United Nations in New York, they are automatically—all member states are obliged under Chapter 7 to freeze those assets immediately, and the key phrase is here, "without delay." Very, very quickly.

Mr. PUTNAM. They are obliged to. Has there been full cooperation with that obligation?

Mr. GLASS. It is very hard to say precisely whether there has been complete and full cooperation. We know that, as Mr. Ross mentioned in his testimony, that 170 countries report that they have issued blocking orders, that they have instructed their financial institutions to freeze assets on given names and specific individuals. We do know, as I mentioned, that assets have been frozen overseas. We make an effort through our embassies to monitor and to find out whether countries are being effective in their efforts.

But there are challenges out there that continue to exist, particularly when you get into less developed areas of the world. It is one thing in the United States for officials here to issue notices to financial institutions to freeze assets, to do that electronically on a real-time basis. It is another to try and imagine this being done in certain parts of Africa or in countries such as Afghanistan.

Mr. PUTNAM. Or Syria or Libya or some of the other helpful countries who are members of the United Nations.

Mr. GLASS. Those present their own unique challenges in their own way. But we do make demarches on a routine basis to the Syrian Government on these issues when a name comes up and is added to the U.N. list.

We do send our diplomats in to request that they also freeze those names, as we do in all other countries with whom we have diplomatic relations. This is new. Our embassies are more engaged in these activities than ever. The instructions that we send out to our posts on this are cleared by all of the agencies in Washington, by the Treasury Department, by the Justice Department, and are coordinated very closely at post. So it is a work in progress. But it is one that we spend an awful lot of effort on. And we have raised, I am completely convinced, the level of international attention to terrorist finance to a level that was never there before.

Mr. PUTNAM. Let me ask just one financial and brief question before I yield back to Mr. Platts. The events of September 11th, I think everybody universally refers to them as this turning point in the way that we have viewed the world or the way that we have approached certain crimes. It has been referred that money laundering is one of them, that it was this watershed event that shifted the way that we viewed the process, the investigation, the procedure.

The Congress reacted, passing the Patriot Act. There were Executive orders, creation of the Department of Homeland Security. So we took this jarring event in the Federal Government's bureaucratic culture that the folks, all of you who have to go out there and have your specific missions—that was a jarring event, followed by several jarring legislative activities, not the least of which was severing your 170-some-odd year relationship with Treasury and putting you into the newly created Department, and moving Customs and things like that. So we have done all of that.

How much better are you able to communicate with all of the other agencies sitting at this table than you were prior to that? Do you have access? For example, Secret Service is here, Customs is here. Do you have complete, unfettered access to each other's data bases when you are involved in an investigation, or are there still barriers to that? And how does that work across the other departments? I would be interested in hearing your thoughts on that.

Mr. TOWNSEND. I will kick off that, Mr. Chairman. With regard to the data bases, on a technical level I believe the answer to that is no. And to some degree that shouldn't come as a surprise to us, because we have spent the last 20 or 30 or 40 years designing things that way. If you look at a very grassroots level, look at the voice radio systems just in emergency first responders.

Some 20 or 30 years ago when I was a uniformed policeman, it was thought to be a bad thing that you could hear everyone's radio traffic in a county area. So we worked for the last 30 years designing stovepiped radio systems where you couldn't hear everything that was going on in a region or a county. That was thought to be a good thing.

Well, we think differently now. So while we recognize that our thinking has to change, unfortunately it is not going to happen overnight.

When you asked the question on the access to everyone's data bases, speaking with the Secret Service and—the U.S. Secret Service relationship is when I need something, we are going to give it to them. There was a boom in technology in terms of the realization that communication has to exist, and that information we have is available to other law enforcement partners. The answer is yes.

I think the answer was yes post-September 11, but it is an emphasis now. Excuse me, pre-September 11. The answer was, yes, pre-September 11. It is an emphatic yes now.

Mr. PUTNAM. Mr. Ross, do you have better coordination with the different agencies today than you did prior?

Mr. ROSS. Well, I would like to give a quick anecdote if I could. Immediately after September 11, at that point I was a DOJ employee. I went over to work with the FBI when they established the precursor to the TFOS, which is called the TFRG, Terrorist Financial Review Group. It was the FBI initiative to create a financing—interagency financing strategy for terrorism. Never been done before.

What happened was, we sat around the table and said, "Who are the best people at agencies to have sitting here with their data bases so that we can immediately plug into them?" The first order of business was, well, who do we need? We need IRS CI. We need FinCEN. We absolutely need Customs. We need DEA. Federal Reserve would be helpful.

And what happened, people came, worked together, shared literally a huge room, everyone with their own data bases. And I have never seen an entity function better. But, at the same time, everyone still maintained separate data bases. Everyone still was patched into their own individual data bases.

Most importantly, everyone brought to the table their own unique abilities with what you do with the data that was being fed to them.

So in answer to your question, I am not sure if it is better. I know better agency coordination on terrorist financing is better—it virtually didn't exist prior to September 11, if it did at all. So it is tremendously better.

Are people more aware? Are they more aware of what data bases can be applied and can be applied on the interagency basis and proactively to identify terror? Yes, an emphatic yes to that. So I think that there are times when an interoperability capability is useful—and at times, even if it is useful, will be made more useful—to have the right people with the right data bases work in an interagency composition, which is what I think is the most effective use of these data bases that exist.

Mr. PUTNAM. Thank you. We will return to this. But I want to yield back to Mr. Platts.

Mr. PLATTS. Thank you, Mr. Chairman. I am going to kind of pick up where Chairman Putnam was with the international community, and probably, Mr. Ross and Mr. Glass, really focus on your testimonies.

As I was preparing for today's hearing, and again having the chance to review your testimonies ahead of time—appreciate you sharing that—there was an article in my Sunday paper yesterday that I read, and you may have seen a variation of it in the Washington paper or elsewhere. I am going to just read a short part of it.

I am quoting from the article, "Governments around the world aren't enforcing global sanctions designed to stem the flow of money to al-Qaeda and impede the business activity of the organization's financiers, allowing the terrorist network to retain formidable financial resources, according to the United States, European and U.N. investigators.

"Several businessmen designated by the United Nations as terrorist financiers, whose assets were supposed to have been frozen more than 2 years ago, continue to run vast business empires and travel freely, because most nations are unaware of the sanctions and others don't enforce them," the investigators said.

"Several charities based in Saudi Arabia and Pakistan that were reportedly shut down by the governments, because of the groups' alleged financial ties to Osama bin Laden, also continue to operate freely," they said.

Then I jump to basically the end of the article that says, "So far the world body has publicly named 272 people as sponsors of terrorism. But U.N./U.S. officials say they don't know where more than half of those people are, and only 83 of 191 countries have submitted the required U.N. reports on attacking terrorist financing and implementing the travel ban. Only a third of those have given a list to their border guards."

That doesn't present the best picture for the world community stepping up to the plate and delivering, as we understand they are obligated to do. And that is kind of following up Chairman Putnam's question of who isn't, in assessing the job they are doing?

And I think, Mr. Glass starting with you, according to this—and I did not have the chance between yesterday morning reading this and this morning to try to verify some of those numbers—but according to this, only 83 of 191 countries have submitted the required U.N. reports. That is something that we should be able to verify. And I would appreciate for the record if the Department of State could provide both of our subcommittees this report that goes to compliance with the obligations that these 191 countries have.

Is that 83 number correct? And who are the other 90 or so that are not submitting the required U.N. reports regarding terrorist financing? From a specific request, I would appreciate that information. That should be readily determinable by the Department.

But I welcome, maybe in a more broad response, of—we never heard any specific nations mentioned. Who has done a great job and who hasn't? And I would like to revisit that, especially in light of, you know, my citizens back home are reading this article. And I appreciate you can't make other countries do what they are obligated to do under their U.N. Charter agreement. But we need to know who those countries are and what can we do as a government to try to get them to do what they are obligated to do as members of the U.N.

Mr. GLASS. Well, thank you. I counted about 10 or 12 questions in there.

Mr. PLATTS. I imagine, at least.

Mr. GLASS. And I am somewhat familiar with this U.N. report that came out about 3 weeks ago. First of all, on the question that governments are not enforcing sanctions around the world it is, at the end of the day, up to each individual country to implement sanctions in accordance with the U.N. resolutions—in accordance with their U.N. obligations.

We, however, in Washington do routinely, through our embassies overseas, remind governments of those obligations. And we do engage them. If we have bilateral discussions with specific governments in Washington, we will make that part of the agenda for discussions, and ask them to tell us how things are going on the terrorist finance front on asset freezing, on travel bans. I would tell you, as part of our talking points when we do discuss terrorist finance, those issues are always prominent, including the travel ban issue, which we have been highlighting more and more as time goes along.

The specific—some of the specific cases mentioned in the U.N. report were referring to the NADA–NASREDDIN network in Europe, which has been one that we and the Treasury and Justice Department have been looking at for quite some time, and we have frozen those names domestically and at the U.N. some time ago now.

We were also intrigued to learn recently, slightly before the press reporting here, of the issue of how some European countries are dealing with the freezing of assets.

And the issue for the Europeans, for some European countries, not all of them, but for some of them is, how you define assets. When you freeze assets are you just talking about bank accounts, or are you taking about material assets, things, an automobile, a building of some kind or another?

And apparently in different European countries they deal with this definition in a legal sense in different ways. And this has become a bigger issue that apparently was featured at a workshop that the European Union held on November 7th, last month. And the Europeans are paying more and more attention to this to try to come to terms with just this issue in response to this question.

You asked about certain charities being frozen around the world. These came up also in that report. And we have been in discussions with both Pakistan and Saudi Arabia both of which you mentioned regarding these charities, regarding the freezing of assets of these charities. But in some cases it is not just a question of freezing the assets of charities inside any one of these countries, since these organizations frequently operate in other countries as well.

And in some cases, freezing assets is not the only action that is to be taken. There are other activities that are taken, such as investigative activities which we are working, as was mentioned, with other countries, investigating charities. There are other methods that are taken such as regulatory oversight. And on other occasions it is not always clear how much wittingness or affiliation has been involved with a charity toward the support of terrorism. But we are very much engaged in that activity and trying to make sure that a charity that is designated is actually frozen, in fact.

You mentioned that—you read that approximately half of the countries around the world were not aware of their obligation to freeze assets, if I understood your question.

Mr. PLATTS. That is what the story states.

Mr. GLASS. I can only confirm to you that we discuss, we raise the U.N. obligation with every country with whom we have diplomatic relations on a regular basis around the world. So if these countries claim they are not aware of their U.N. obligations, the United States has reminded them of those U.N. obligations on a regular and repeated basis.

Some of the countries around the world give the lists to their border guards. This is also something that we remind them too, that there is a travel ban. We remind countries of this, that there is a travel sanction that comes with the U.N. obligations here. We have confirmed, for example, that in rather out-of-the-way places, in Asia, countries have told us, for example, that, they don't have the capability always to freeze assets in all of their banks, because their banks often conduct business on the basis of hand receipts, for example.

But they do pass out the lists to their border guards and do use them in terms of travel bans, which some countries do, some don't.

We would like to know more about those countries that don't, because we think it is important that they do, that they be reminded of that. And we will make efforts to do so in the future.

In terms of completing reports to the United Nations, the actual U.N. report which is in, I believe it is on the U.N. Web site—I am told it is at this point in time—does list by name those countries that have not submitted reports to the U.N. in compliance with the 1267 Committee at this point in time. So you can get that list off of the U.N. If you don't have it, I am sure we can also get it and provide it to you.

My brief scanning of that list of names earlier, I don't have this report with me here, indicated to me that many of those countries are in lesser developed areas that are not perhaps part of the mainstream financial system that we always—that we think of when we think of banks and bank regulations. But, nonetheless, we think it is important that all countries report to the U.N. on this very important issue.

Which countries so far have done a good job and which have not? I think there is a lot to be done for all of us. I do know that, for example, that the European Union has put together its own mechanisms for listing names, for adding names very, very quickly, that are designated by the United Nations, so that all European Union member states are required to freeze assets when names are added to the U.N. list.

Other countries around the world have what we call self-executing mechanisms, where as soon as a name is added to the U.N. list, in those countries, it automatically becomes regulation or law to freeze those assets in financial institutions, and those countries are required to freeze immediately as well.

Other countries are less responsive and may not have such quick responsiveness on those names. We would encourage them, however, to improve that. And as part of that, we have a team, we have several teams actually that travel around the world trying to provide countries with the technical capabilities to freeze assets in order to carry out these obligations, to get them capabilities to buildup not only a suspicious activity reporting mechanism, but also a mechanism to notify their banks of names that should be frozen, to provide identifying information, to search for bank accounts.

But I will tell you that in my own work on this issue over the past 2½ years, it has struck me how challenging this can be in some countries. If I take, for example, just the country of Afghanistan and try to think about how to implement sanctions in that country, it became very clear, for example, that Afghan citizens almost routinely do not know their own dates of birth. They may know the year in which they were born, but there is no central registry for the day and month when Afghan citizens were born.

So you have to ask yourself, if you are going to identify accounts, if you are going to ask banking or financial institutions to freeze assets and you don't have a date of birth of an individual, it becomes very, very difficult to do so, because there are a lot of people with names that are very, very similar.

Frequently also we only have one part, a fragment of a name that we are dealing with when we are trying to freeze assets. And that leads to the comment that you also find in the U.N. report, which is an accurate comment, that identifying information is not adequate. And it is not. It is a constant quest that we, that OFAC, that the Treasury Department, that the intelligence and law enforcement community are constantly challenged with, to come up with specific identifying information in order that we can be effective and freeze assets and not, for example, inform financial institutions to freeze the assets of someone named Smith, which is a worthless exercise, because you get so many positive hits that you really can't be effective.

These are the challenges that we are facing. We are getting better. And we are getting better with countries around the world. But we have a long way to go. And part of that, an important part of that, which I think is supported nicely by the Congress, is providing technical assistance, helping other countries to come to terms in their financial networks with building systems to actually freeze assets and identify people.

Mr. PLATTS. Well, I appreciate the substantive answer, and trying to touch on the various points. And I would agree, one, that we are seeing headway and we are making headway and seeing progress. And I would agree there are differences and challenges from a Third World country trying to fulfill these requirements versus the United States or the European Union or other more developed, wealthier countries.

But I guess what I would hope, and we certainly can pull up the list from the U.N. site that is specifically referenced in the report, but I would still appreciate the Department of State providing these subcommittees a list of those nations that the Department identifies—and the best way I can say, is where there is an identified charity, where there isn't a question of misidentification, but this is the charity in question, and there is a sizable amount that is to be frozen, and for whatever reason that host nation is not freezing, that we have a best picture possible of who is fulfilling the U.N. requirements and who is not.

And it really goes to one of the frustrations that I think a lot of people feel about the U.N. And one of the reasons I am grateful for the leader that we have in the White House is we have a President that said the U.N. needs to—what it says needs to mean something. If there is no action, the words are meaningless. And with Iraq for, what, 16 or 17 times we said, do this or else, and we never acted. And thanks to our President, the Prime Minister of Great Britain, and others who joined us, there was action to followup those words and enforce those words.

And my worry is that we are seeing something similar here. We have all of these countries agreeing in word to do this. But the question: Are they really doing it? Are there actions that are coming about because of those words? And I would be interested in seeing which nations aren't. If it is a Saudi Arabia or a Germany, that is different than if it is an Afghanistan, given Afghanistan is, as we speak, trying to craft a new constitution. But I think that would help our perspective at the Congress.

A couple of specific questions. And, Mr. Ross, I do want to allow you to comment as well. But on the U.N. definition of assets and the debate out there, I take it that there is no definition in the U.N. regarding the freezing of assets? And that is the reason for the disparity—or is it—there is a definition in the U.N. requirements, and countries are choosing then to actually enforce it differently?

Mr. GLASS. The Security Council resolution that uses the word "assets" does not provide a more specific definition.

Mr. PLATTS. OK.

Mr. GLASS. To the best of my knowledge.

Mr. PLATTS. OK. Thank you. I guess the information that would be helpful is the Department has identified who you go back to. If you could share that with us, I would appreciate that. That you know are not doing it; that you are having your representatives at the embassies go out and remind them of their obligation.

Mr. GLASS. Could I just add that the Department does not maintain a list of countries, for example, that are more cooperative or less cooperative or anything like that. We do try to encourage, with every country with whom we work around the world, that they take their various obligations in the realm of terrorist finance seriously and implement the Security Council resolutions. But also—and this is something that is much broader than just the State Department, but it affects all of us here at the table—is how they are cooperating with us, for example, at an investigative level on a certain name or a target or issue, or how they cooperate with us in auditing books or quietly providing records, for example, bank records in one case or another.

So it is a very broad effort. And I just wanted to——

Mr. PLATTS. Right. And probably a give-and-take as you look at all of those aspects. I appreciate that. I guess to best possibly refine my request is, to go back to that, where there is an absolutely known charity with these assets in this country that is party to that U.N. Charter, and the Department is aware that they are not freezing those assets, that be shared with the subcommittees.

And, Mr. Ross, I don't know if you want to add. Mr. Glass covered it probably pretty extensively.

Mr. ROSS. Mr. Glass has covered it very well. I do note for the record, I believe, in that article my superior did also point out the issues with respect to the legal and regulatory and structural problem about what is an asset in some of the countries.

Mr. PLATTS. Maybe if you could followup—or jointly—another specific, that apparently is going to be an identified listing of countries. We talked about the 191 having the obligation. And, Mr. Ross, you referenced 172 that have blocking orders in force.

So there is 19 that, you know, are identifiable as not having blocking orders, of those 191. If we could have that shared with us, that would be great.

If I can touch on one other issue quickly, and then send it back to you, Mr. Chairman.

One is just the testimony. I appreciate a number of you talking about the Patriot Act. And I think, Mr. Whitehead, your statement sums it up, I think very importantly, for the public to understand the importance of that legislation and this battle against terrorism, and your quote, past terrorist financing methods—I am sorry, I am reading the wrong sentence. "The success in preventing another catastrophic attack on the United States homeland would have been much more difficult if not impossible without the act." And I appreciate your highlighting in some detail, as a number of you did in your written testimony, that the Patriot Act has gone a long way to giving you the tools of the 21st century to protect Americans here at home.

And, you know, through this hearing, help the public to understand that there is a lot of misinformation, you know, or misunderstanding out there about the Patriot Act and how it impacts Americans versus allowing you to go after the bad guys. And I appreciate your specifically talking about it, as well as others, in your testimony; that has benefited this law enforcement effort.

Thank you, Mr. Chairman.

Mr. PUTNAM. Thank you, Mr. Platts.

I want to return to Mr. Glass, if I may. You have represented your Department exceptionally well and been a very good diplomat. But you are the Director of the Office of Economic Sanctions Policy, and you have survived two different waves of questioning with only a passing reference to one continent.

Surely you can give us some sense of those nations. You have already quantified it by saying that a third of the frozen assets are in the United States and two-thirds are abroad. Of those two-thirds of the assets that are abroad, where are they concentrated? What are the top two, three, five places where these other frozen foreign assets are located, as some way of giving us a better understanding of which nations are the source of the greatest volume of funds for terrorists?

Mr. GLASS. Mr. Chairman, I would have to defer to my—or perhaps invite my Treasury colleague to comment on this, because the data on which those conclusions are based is data that is compiled by the Department of the Treasury.

They do have, as best they can put together, an indication as to which countries compile a certain amount of information on what assets are frozen. Some of that information is subject to various bank secrecy issues in those countries. And it is not State Department data. But nonetheless it does, I think, reflect some of the efforts.

The one comment I would make is that my own viewing of that information seems to indicate that a lot of those assets are in places where money would normally pass through; that is, large banking centers, large financial centers around the world. But I don't know if, Jeff, you are in a position to——

Mr. ROSS. Bob, appreciate the hand-off. Of course, what I will do, Mr. Chairman, is I did not come prepared to identify countries. I will go back, and the Treasury Department will address this as a followup question, with respect to countries and freezing.

One thing I cannot recall is if there are any restrictions on disclosure of the specific amounts by country. But if there are, obviously we will work very closely with the subcommittee to get you the information.

Mr. PUTNAM. How about Customs? Who has been the most cooperative, and who has been the least cooperative in dealing with the post-September 11 changes that have occurred as we attempt to crack down on the terrorism financing and other money laundering and smuggling and things of that nature?

Ms. FORMAN. Well, I can just address the countries we are dealing with in terms of the money laundering arena and some of the terrorist financing arena. In terms of the money laundering, drug money laundering in particular, we have an excellent relationship with the Colombian Government.

Under Plan Colombia, we have several initiatives that have been put in place to address the black market peso exchange and narcotics money laundering. In regards to money laundering and terrorist financing, we work very closely with our Canadian counterparts, British counterparts, and various other European countries around the world. And we have had great success in that area.

Mr. PUTNAM. For any of you, how cooperative have countries outside of Western Europe been, particularly those nations in Southern Asia and the Middle East and Africa? Understandably we are dealing with countries that do have less developed financial institutions, less developed regulatory frameworks.

But I think what the two of us are struggling to grasp is, is the conventional wisdom correct that a substantial portion of the funding is coming from Saudi Arabia or is it not? Are our allies in Western Europe cooperating with us as strongly in the boardrooms and the banking houses of Antwerp and London and Paris as they are in other parts of the world militarily and diplomatically, or is there a gap there?

Are the European financial centers—you are the former Consul General to Bern, Switzerland—are the Swiss banking houses cooperative, relatively speaking, or are they not? And I can't think of any other ways to ask the same question. But perhaps you all might help illuminate this a bit for the benefit of the public forum, rather than a memo to us in 2 weeks that we read and glean the information that we need from, but essentially the purpose of a congressional field hearing, getting out of Washington and into the Tampa, FLs or the York, PAs of the world would be lost.

So if you would, please help us understand better just how cooperative these other nations have been. For example, you mentioned the U.N. Web site that lists those countries participating. But in response to a number of Mr. Platts's questions, you correctly included the caveat that we remind, we work with, we encourage. We coerce. We incent those nations with whom we have diplomatic relations.

Now, how many countries do we have diplomatic relations with that are members of the United Nations, and how many are members of the U.N. but do not enjoy official diplomatic relations with the United States. That may be a back channel for all of those funds, because we don't have relations, we don't have embassies, we don't have official ties that would allow us to encourage, incent, and coerce?

Mr. GLASS. Generally speaking, Mr. Chairman, those countries with whom we don't have diplomatic relations are for the most part those countries that are state sponsors of terrorism with whom we have no financial or banking relationships either, and we should not have any kind of financial interaction. And these are closely regulated and enforced by the U.S. Government.

To address your question, if I might just try to take a stab at it, as to how cooperation is going around the world on terrorist finance, I think you rightfully noted that we have good cooperation with European Union member states. We talk to the Europeans on a regular basis. They have—not only do they have a mechanism for designating names from the United Nations, an automatic self-executing mechanism, but they also maintain a clearinghouse list for non-al-Qaeda-linked names that do not go to the U.N.

These are also terrorist names, but they are not linked to al-Qaeda or the Taliban. That list has, and I don't have it with me today, but it has about 110, 120 names on it that have come from various corners of the world. There is an International Sikh group that is listed there. There are ETA names that are listed on that list. And the Europeans, when they add names to that list, they come to us and ask us to freeze those names as well on our list in the United States, which we do. These are names, as I mentioned, which do not qualify for asset freeze at the United Nations because of the way that the Security Council resolutions are written to focus primarily on al-Qaeda.

Cooperation with the Europeans is good. I am happy to discuss that more if you want more detail there. But let me move on to some of the other regions.

In the Middle East, cooperation varies from country to country. Around the Persian Gulf, we have had a number of very promising joint efforts with a number of countries there that have, for example, provided a large number of banking records in some cases. In other cases, they have conducted raids and shut down Hawala organizations. They have held conferences on Hawalas in order encourage countries throughout the region to implement regulatory measures to control Hawalas that have been very successful, that have resonated widely.

They have frozen assets of individuals and entities in their countries. The situation with Saudi Arabia, which I provided more detail of in my testimony, is one that is a very important focus for the United States. We are in regular high-level contact with the Saudi Government. Just several months ago, there was created an—under the leadership of the FBI, a joint task force with Saudi officials. I don't know if my colleague wishes to discuss more about that, but that has been mentioned in previous testimony. That is a very promising and very effective operation where we, U.S. investigators and Saudi Arabia investigators on the ground, are working full time to followup terrorist leads, including in the fields of terrorist finance.

The Saudis have joined us in designating key Saudi financiers. They have joined us in designating some branches of al Haramain. There have been discussions with the Saudis about broader efforts against al Haramain, as well as other charities that are promising. But I don't—in this forum I am not in a position to get into the specifics of what we plan to do in the future with specific targets.

Cooperation is improving. There is more to do. But it is improving and we are, we believe, seeing results. The Saudis have frozen assets of terrorists and terrorist supporters inside Saudi Arabia. Again, I don't know if I am in a position to share that information in this forum or not.

In the case of Pakistan, a very important country as well, we have had ongoing discussions with the Pakistanis. The Secretary of the Treasury visited Pakistan in August or September of this year where there was discussion of terrorism finance. There are very important charities and organizations in Pakistan whose assets have been frozen, but there is a lot more in that country that needs to be done. We do have, however, a good working relationship with that country.

In Asia, there has been a lot of terrorist activity in Asia, particularly by Jemaah Islamiyah. When we and 49 other countries submitted Jemaah Islamiyah to the U.N. for asset freezing I believe back in October 2002, it was the largest such effort against any organization by an international coalition, 50 countries asking the U.N. to designate and freeze this organization. That has taken place.

And since that time, some additional 22 individuals have been added to the U.N. list. These are key financial people, financial and other leaders of Jemaah Islamiyah in Asia, and Asian countries are obliged to freeze assets of these individuals. Whether they have, and to what extent, depends in this case particularly to the degree as to whether they have the technical expertise to actually implement financial freezes. This is something where we are providing technical assistance and advice to several of these countries in Asia at this time in order to help build that capacity, to help them in this regard.

And so there is an effort, there are cooperative efforts with countries going on.

We have ongoing dialogs as well with Russia, with China, where they freeze assets. At least they tell us they do. We are not exactly sure how they go about this or how they implement freeze orders domestically in their individual systems. But we are told by their officials, by various parts of their governments, that they implement freeze orders.

In other countries around the world, they will either tell us that they are implementing freeze orders, or they will request additional expertise and technical assistance to do so. But as I said, this is—this is something we are continuing to work at, where we do approach these governments on a routine basis. We do encourage them. And when they ask for technical assistance, we try to assist in that regard, and provide that expertise.

Mr. PUTNAM. Thank you, Mr. Glass.

Mr. Whitehead, my financial question is for you. You have dodged most of the bullets today. As someone who has been in the Washington office and in field offices all around the country, we would certainly presume, or at least hope that the benefits of the successive waves of legislation benefit the field offices the most.

We hear a great deal from local law enforcement that there is insufficient information sharing. And at the Federal Government alone, we have a small slice of the different agencies and departments that also must share information critical to your successful outcome in an investigation.

So my question to you would be, have you seen an improvement in information sharing, or are there still barriers because of security clearances, data base incapabilities, lack of interoperability? Are there still barriers, or has your ability to get your hands on all of the evidence, all of the information that the entire Federal Government has collected that may be of interest to you in your specific circumstance, is it where it ought to be?

Mr. WHITEHEAD. Well, thank you for giving me the opportunity to answer your last question here. There has been tremendous improvement since September 11 in that arena. Our JTTFs, with having representatives of all of the Federal agencies as well as local and State representatives working hand in hand every day, has tremendously improved the flow of intelligence.

We have had tremendous successes in the integration. As Mr. Ross stated yesterday, or earlier, it is very effective to have those data bases available. Although they don't talk to each other, we have them colocated under one roof so that we can have access to all of those data bases, and that has been tremendously helpful to us.

So the legislation that has been passed, that the Patriot Act has given us, is a tremendous tool in order to combat this problem. Probably one of the biggest examples of that here in Tampa, of course, is the al-Arian case, where we now, because of the wall going down between the classified and criminal side, we were able to use 9 years of gathered intelligence to support that criminal prosecution. So that is just a tremendous advantage for us.

Mr. PUTNAM. That was as a result of the Patriot Act? Correct?

Mr. WHITEHEAD. Exactly. Because of the removal of the wall between the intelligence and criminal side which previously prohibited using that type of intelligence to support a criminal investigation, we were unable to do that. But now we are able to successfully support these cases. And this is an excellent example of how we have been able to use that as a result of the act. So this allowed the use of national security letters, which enabled us to obtain records, to gather intelligence in these cases has been tremendously helpful; prior to the act, we would have to obviously go to a court to get some type of court order in order to obtain their financial records or telephone records in these classified cases.

And now we are able to do that on a national security letter, on my signature. So it has just been a tremendously helpful process to help us gather the intelligence we need to prevent acts of terrorism from occurring.

Mr. PUTNAM. Thank you, Mr. Whitehead.

Mr. Platts, do you have any final thoughts or last questions?

Mr. PLATTS. If I could try to run through some real quick. And if it is OK, I would like to reserve the ability to submit some for the record.

Mr. PUTNAM. Certainly. We will be making that motion at the end.

Mr. PLATTS. OK. A final comment on Chairman Putnam and I both kind of pursuing the country issue and, I think, trying to summarize for why we see it as so important, for two primary reasons. One is the importance of this effort being comprehensive. You know, if 150 countries are doing a great job and 41 are not, we know where the terrorists are going to put all of their money. They are going to put it in the 41 that are not.

And so, you know, the importance of us encouraging every nation to do what they have agreed to do, and again for the U.N. to mean something, if they are part of that agreement they need to comply with what they agreed to. And if they don't, it just—we know where the terrorists are going to go with those resources.

The second is, you know, our Nation is a very generous Nation, and we have always been a beacon of hope for people coming here. But we have also been the beacon of hope for our willingness to go to other countries and provide assistance. And I think it is appropriate for taxpayers to know if a country is in need of assistance, humanitarian, health care, education, whatever it may be, and American taxpayers step up to the plate and say we are going to help, that we don't want to be doing that for a nation that is not helping us.

And if there is a nation that is on their list saying, no we won't freeze those assets, well, that is fine. But don't look for America to, you know, come helping you and your citizens. And that is something that as policymakers in Congress we need to know. And that is something that would reflect—be reflected in the actions Congress takes when we pass appropriations bills. And those countries need to understand that our generosity maybe won't continue if they are not helping us to track down criminals, which is what we are after.

So I think it is important to kind of phrase those two priorities as to why we kind of have to continue to seek some specifics. I will try to run through two or three items real quickly here and not get into as in depth as we have these other issues.

One. Mr. Ross, just for the volume of information, and as we have changed the statute and regs regarding suspicious activity reports the volume that you are now handling has grown dramatically. Can you quickly summarize, one, from the technology standpoint, which relates to out of the subcommittee, your ability to use technology. From a funding standpoint, do you have the resources from Congress to assimilate this information you get; are you just doing the best you can, but there is no way you can handle all you are getting?

Mr. ROSS. Thank you, Mr. Chairman. I think, particularly from a financing perspective, that they are doing a much better job of using technology, particularly in the area of link analysis, which is data mining, which is a crucial area where what you do is you take disparate pieces of information; for instance in the SAR data base, in the narrative text, it could mention this phone number here, in another field on another SAR filed in a whole another place, that could mention the same phone number there. There are no linkages whatsoever between those two.

However, if you purchase the right software and you apply the right package, through a link analysis you will find a commonalty between those phone numbers, telephone records, common addresses, common bank accounts. That type of approach is what is being utilized by FinCEN now. That approach is being used in the proactive reports that they are sending out to law enforcement. And I think I gave the statistics on the numbers, and the hundreds of those that have been sent out to law enforcement, quite a few implicating possible terrorist financing activities.

So what we are doing is using existing and new technologies better to link financial data to get to the investigators who can then use that data to try to make their investigations. So I think we are comfortable.

Mr. PLATTS. Are you strained from a human resource standpoint or financial resources in applying that technology?

Mr. ROSS. No, I don't believe we are. I would defer to a FinCEN specialist. I would have to get back with FinCEN. But from what I have seen, the numbers and quality of the reports going out are holding steady. What is more remarkable to me is the FinCEN ability to communicate with 29,000 financial institutions on these 314a requests that are coming in from law enforcement. Now, they are very refined. Those requests only can be made with respect to terrorist financing, and in the most significant money laundering cases.

But as a result of those, as I believe I testified, there have been indictments, at least in part based on the responses from the financial institutions. There have been hundreds, I think, of grand jury subpoenas for the bank accounts. There have been thousands of tips and leads.

So the technology now that is being applied—5 years ago I would have told you this is impossible, it can't be done—and today it is being done on a biweekly basis.

Mr. PLATTS. Great. I am going to touch real quickly on two others. One that concerns me is the decision by Treasury on the Mexican Matricular Consular card being used for opening bank accounts as an acceptable means of identification.

My understanding is Department of Justice, FBI, and perhaps the Secret Service don't support that decision to allow that as a form of identification because of the ease of which they can be acquired. If you would want to comment in defense of the Treasury, and if FBI and Secret Service, or if any of our panelists want to comment on your position.

Mr. ROSS. Thank you, Mr. Chairman. Yes, I will comment on this. We at Treasury decided that the financial institutions—and I think an important thing to remember is that we are not talking exclusively about banks here, we are speaking of security brokers, mutual funds, brokerage houses, future commission markets. We are talking about a wide range of financial institutions that do business in a wide variety of capacities. This is not just a simple banking community.

For risk-based analysis, what we have mandated, and we put out final regs in May 2003, are that these financial institutions must have written policies and procedures, a basis—which provides a reasonable basis for them to conclude that they are aware of the identity of the person with whom they are doing the business.

We are aware of the concern with respect to Matriculars. We are aware of concerns probably with respect to driver's licenses, for instance.

Mr. PLATTS. That is my last question. I was going to touch on that.

Mr. ROSS. I think any and all identification instruments can be abused. There is no question about that. The question—our view at Treasury is that the financial institution itself, the one that has created the environment in which it operates and the one that is providing the service, has to be the one that is in—from a reasonable perspective, the best position to identify what is reasonable for them to have to identify the person with whom they are transacting business.

Mr. PLATTS. But if our Federal Government is saying that this other Federal Government's official identification is acceptable—I mean, that we recognize it—who is the bank then to say, no, we are not going to recognize the Mexican Consulate's identification they have provided? I mean, it really to me falls to us to say is that acceptable or not, that specific form; as opposed to having, how many institutions did you—the tens of thousands, you know, to have all of them individually saying, this is acceptable. It worries me, because when we are trying to have that comprehensive effort, we have a gaping, you know, hole here that a terrorist can get through, because of how easily these identifications can be acquired.

Mr. ROSS. Well, as I said, we are aware of the concerns. We do not believe that we have sufficient discrete information to suggest that a particular item of identity is more likely not to be accurately either attained or to have accurate information on it than other items of information.

The problem with trying to identify—trying to use a regulation such as 326 where you are going after a wide variety of financial institutions offering a wide variety of services is if you try go down the path and say this is good, this is bad, you are going to end up with a regulation that is constantly going to tend to morph and to be changed.

We are trying to work a regulation that allows—reasonably allows us to be able to identify who the account holders were. And we understand that there are differences of opinion on this point.

Mr. PLATTS. If I can wrap up with the FBI and Secret Service on that specifically. Do you believe that we should continue to allow this form of identification to be accepted? And related to it, regarding driver's licenses, should we at the Federal level prohibit individuals who are not legally present in the United States to have driver's licenses, given how they are accepted as an official form of identification? So that—two different issues, but very much related to who is this person and are they who they say they are, and are they here lawfully?

Mr. WHITEHEAD. Well, clearly the use of fraudulent identifications is a major problem for us in these investigations and has unfortunately been one that is difficult to get our arms around as far as constantly trying to identify individuals and developing intelligence on it.

As far as the position on whether we agree with the use of these cards or not, we are going to have to defer to my national office TFOS, to give you any current positions from headquarters.

Mr. FABIAN. Actually, I don't know if I can speak to that issue. I don't know if I can address that issue specifically. I would say that all of us here at the table, I am sure all of us on the panel recognize that the purpose of having identification when opening accounts, conducting financial transactions, that there is a reasonable expectation that information is correct and legitimate.

In fact, the Patriot Act strengthened the ability of the banks to determine those that were opening accounts and requires specific information. So I think any——

Mr. PLATTS. I guess if we could whether—which of you would maybe followup is what is the FBI's official position specifically on Matriculars; you know, should they be allowed as an acceptable form of identification for opening up a bank account in that—by the Federal Government?

Mr. FABIAN. I am sorry.

Mr. PLATTS. If we can have that followup to the subcommittee, that would get to the exact point. With the Secret Service?

Mr. TOWNSEND. With your permission, we would submit for the record on that issue. With regard to the driver's license issue, if I can parcel your question with regard to the possession, we will also submit for the record on that.

But I would like to let the subcommittee, the chairmen know, that the Secret Service has an ongoing initiative with the American Association for Motor Vehicle Administrators, the Document Security Alliance, to continue to address this issue of our 50 different driver's licenses and the attendant problems.

It is something that we think we can bring some expertise to with regard to our document analysis capabilities. And it is something that is ongoing. We meet with those associates regularly. It is something that we recognize as a real concern. We are endeavoring to bring the technology that is available into driver's licenses.

And, of course, as you are aware, you are dealing with 50 separate State legislatures. It is not something that is going to be an overnight fix. But these two organizations, AMVA and the Document Security Alliance, I think it is a good partnership. And the issue that you bring up is one that is at the forefront.

Mr. PLATTS. I appreciate it. That gets to that second part, coming out of the State house myself, and Adam as well, in having that uniformity. And if there is guidance from your work with the national association, of the State administrators, the highway administrators, that we need legislation, legislation that would through Federal funding help provide that, you know, coordination and that uniform driver's license so we have the ability for one State to better talk to another, that this guy has already got a license here and not let him get five other ones in different States.

We would welcome that feedback if you believe that, as you are working with the association, there is a need for a legislative approach. Because I support that effort. And having that uniformity would be very helpful. I appreciate your both following up with specifics on the driver's license and the Matriculars.

And, Mr. Chairman, I just want to thank you for your patience with me, as I do have more questions, but I will submit those for the record to followup.

And again I appreciate our witnesses and your allowing me to join you at this hearing today.

Mr. PUTNAM. Thank you, Mr. Platts. I also have a number of questions. And that being the case, since there are questions that we did not have time for today, the record will remain open for 2 weeks for submitted questions and answers. And we appreciate the panelists' full cooperation in responding.

I want to thank you, Mr. Platts and your staff, as well as the staff of the Subcommittee on Technology for putting together this hearing. It is always a challenge to organize a field hearing outside of Washington with the logistics.

And I appreciate the witnesses cooperating as well as with their travel schedules. We want to thank you for all of your participation. Agencies and law enforcement have a tremendous task before them. I think that we clearly have made progress, but there is also still room for improvement.

As we have discovered in other areas of the Federal Government, grappling with the coordinating efforts and communicating vital information between agencies is an important component to our eventual success.

Without that cooperation on all levels, our goal of choking off terrorist financial networks will be difficult to realize.

With that, we appreciate the participation of the audience. And we certainly want to thank the Port Authority … ration in allowing us to use … eorge W…

… was a…